ONE PERFECT DAUGHTER

HE WAS THE PERFECT SON. UNTIL SHE WASN'T.

JANE FOSTER

One Perfect Daughter:
He Was The Perfect Son. Until She Wasn't
© Jane Foster 2024

ISBN: 978-1-923163-52-2 (Paperback)

A catalogue record for this book is available from the National Library of Australia

Cover Design: Jane Foster and Clark & Mackay
Format and Typeset: Jane Foster and Clark & Mackay
Self-Published by Jane Foster and Clark & Mackay

Proudly printed in Australia by Clark & Mackay

For the real Jules and River. For all your diversities,
idiosyncrasies, strength and brilliance.
I love you both with all my heart, always.

A mother is the truest friend we have. When trials heavy and sudden fall upon us; when adversity takes the place of prosperity; when friends desert us; when trouble thickens around us; still will she cling to us and endeavour by her kind precepts and counsels to dissipate the clouds of darkness and cause peace to return to our hearts.

—Anonymous

PROLOGUE

I sit there in the front row of the graduation assembly. The whole school is there.

There must be over 1,500 boys sitting on the ground in front of us.

The names get called for the top performing boys in year 12.

'Julian Foster,' the headmaster calls

He is the third highest-performing student for his school for the year.

I sit there beaming. I cannot be prouder of my beautiful boy.

He shakes hands with the headmaster and stands in the front row of the eight boys who have worked so hard to be part of the '95 ATAR club'.

I look at his beautiful face and can't believe that I have raised such a warm, caring, intelligent kid.

He stands there looking at me and smiling. I look back at my clever, amazing son and smile back at him.

JANE 2021

I want to die.

Please, God, let me. Why do other people die and I live? I don't want to live anymore.

Jules is not my son anymore. She is my daughter!

This doesn't happen to me. This happens to a friend of a friend's son. A celebrity on TV. The person who lives down the next street. It doesn't happen to me. To my family. To my son!

It's her fault! She has made him do this!

That bitch is the common denominator in all of this!

If she hadn't come along, then he wouldn't have felt depressed. He wouldn't have become anorexic! He wouldn't have become a girl!

I sob and sob and sob! I can't live this life. Please let me have a heart attack, God. Please, please, please?

God, if you just give me one thing in this lifetime, please make it death. My death!

THE BEGINNING

1999

Julian was born on a beautiful day in September 1999. He was a beautiful-looking boy who had the whitest hair and the most brilliant blue eyes.

I fell in love head first.

I really wanted a boy when I was pregnant, and I prayed that I got one. Of course, if it was a girl, I would still have been happy, but ultimately, I wanted a boy.

I never found out the gender when I was pregnant, but I knew if it was a boy, his name would be Julian.

I was about to burst at nearly 42 weeks, but he refused to come out. After a long, drawn-out 28 hours in labour, he came out, slightly blue, and screamed at me, as all babies do.

My friend Suze was also pregnant and due one month after me. We would talk and laugh about how we were not going to have any drugs or any pain relief like morphine or gas or, worst of all, an epidural!

We both were going to have natural births.

As I was into about the 14th hour of labour and vomiting through every contraction and still not even fully dilated, the nurse frankly told me, 'You are not going to get a medal for not having pain relief.'

'Okay,' I decided. 'Give me the epidural!'

As soon as I had given birth, I told Suze, 'Get an epidural straight away!'

She gave birth a month later to a beautiful little girl. We would push our prams down the street and walk for hours while either one of the babies, or both, would be screaming or crying. We would try to ignore it and keep walking. We were doting mothers who were so excited about our babies, but like all mothers, we were exhausted, tired and very, very sleep deprived.

I didn't suffer from post-partum depression but had my moments where I thought I wouldn't cope much longer if Julian kept screaming and crying at me all the time. All I could think about was sleep.

We had a few funny moments when Kevin and I, and Suze and Matt, were first-time parents. Once I just wanted to go out away from everyone and go and shop for clothes and have lunch and do all that stuff that becomes too hard to do when you have a baby around. I remember being at the shops and Kevin phoning me, saying he and Matt were trying to figure out how to change the nappy. I mean, these guys were both successful in their chosen field of work, but they couldn't work that out? I was not in the laughing mood for that, just terribly frustrated!

Another time, Kevin was in the upstairs bedroom with Julian and Matt, and they were chatting. I had the baby monitor on downstairs and was having a drink with one of their other friends David. Kevin and Matt thought it would be pretty funny to say what a prick David was.

They knew the baby monitor was on, and it was a pretty funny moment.

JULES'S INFANCY

Fuck me! Does this kid ever stop screaming? It seems like years have gone by, and he still screams. He has just turned two, and like all first mothers, I want to dress him up and take him to kids' parties and show him off. He does, however, do a lot of screaming. The other kids don't seem to do that, but maybe it's just me because I'm so exhausted.

I am still trying to work a couple of days a week, as my husband and I own a mechanical workshop. I still have to go in and do books and invoicing and payroll and all the stuff you need to do to run a business. My mother and mother-in-law take turns to look after Jules, and one day a week, I put him in a creche. He hates the creche and makes this known to me by screaming and crying every time I leave him there. He also does this at the gym creche when I leave him in there. He screams the house down, and I can hear him from inside the gym. I try to ignore it and know that one day it will stop.

I love all the time I get to spend with him, though. My girlfriend Janine had a baby a year after I did. She had a little girl, and she named her Dani. We would get together once a week for the kids to have a play. We would go down at the park or to one of the play factories and try to tire them out so that they will have a nap in the afternoon. This is when we like to get the wine out and have a glass or two. I need the wine to make me chill. I need it more now that I am a mother. Well, that's what I tell myself.

JULES'S CHILDHOOD

I couldn't decide what school to enrol Jules in when it was nearing the time of him being four. I thought maybe one of the alternate schools or maybe a Catholic school. We weren't religious ourselves; in fact, my husband is quite the 'atheist'. I am of the Church of England and did do the whole church thing when I was younger, but once I got to about nine or ten, my mother asked me if I still wanted to go, and I said, 'No.'

I continued to believe in God, though, but not in the church.

When Jules was around three and a half, we were just about ready to move into our new house that we had just built. It was a drama from the start, and about six weeks away from it being finished, the builder went broke. It was such an ordeal, but luckily, the place we were staying in was now the place that my brother-in-law owned. We sold it to him when we bought the other block to build on. As it turned out, the house took over three years to be completed. It was a nightmare!

I was moving some stuff around the back of the new house when a lady popped her head over the fence. 'Hi,' she said. 'I'm Chrissy.' Before I could say anything, she said, 'Do you have kids?'

'Yes, just the one. His name is Julian.'

'Oh my god,' said Chrissy. 'I have a Julian too.'

'How old?' I asked her.

As it turns out, both the Julians were the same age, and she also had an older son called Joel. In the years to come, we took turns having dinner at each other's houses at least twice a week, and the boys all got on famously. Her husband Brad ended up putting in a secret gate—as we called it—at the back of the two houses so the boys could come and go as much as they pleased. We had such fun times together. Kevin and Brad got along so well. Brad was one of those people that were so likeable you couldn't not like them!

Chrissy was the one that suggested that I should try and enrol in one of the local schools that her boys were going to. I thought it might be a bit hard for my Julian to get into as it was very small, and they only had a small selection of kids that are accepted if they are not Catholic.

As luck would have it, Julian got in there. I think it might have been to do with the fact that Chrissy's boys were at the school and she put in a good word for me.

Jules continued to be friends with Julian and Joel right throughout his childhood. Brad passed away when the boys were just ten and eight. It was such a sad time for everyone involved, and Chrissy and her boys were devastated as they would be. We were all devastated. Why would God take such a vibrant and beautiful man from the world at such a young age? He was just 38 years old.

Chrissy had to go back to work full time them to try and support the boys on her own. I tried to help as much as I could by picking up the boys from school and making them all dinner. I did this a few times a week, as Chrissy was working very long hours and was still trying to cope with the grief of losing her beloved husband. At this time in my life, I became very close to the boys, and the two Julians were inseparable. I had to make sure I called her Julian by his full name and started calling my Julian 'Jules' so they would know which one I was talking to. They used to call themselves the real Triple J like JJJ the radio station, but they liked their version better.

Chrissy ended up being not only one of my best friends but my sister-in-law as well. She ended up marrying my brother-in-law several years later, so now Julian and Joel are my nephews.

JULES'S ADOLESCENCE

Julian hit high school age, and we were unsure whether to send him to an arty sort of high school or to the Catholic boy's college where all his friends were going. He was adamant that he wanted to go to the boy's school as that was where all his friends were going.

I ended up getting him christened Catholic, as I thought this would be easier for the enrolment process at the time.

The priest who was with the school gave me an enlightening lecture on how I shouldn't be christening my son Catholic for education purposes. As he was carrying onto me about this I thought, *Stuff this, I will go and pay another priest somewhere else to do it.*

As I was leaving, he then turned to me and said he would do it.

So Julian was christened Catholic at the ripe old age of 11 so that he would be accepted into the college. The priest turned up late for the christening, drunk, and with half his lunch down his face. I paid him $150 in an envelope for his time.

So, Jules began high school. Like I mentioned before, he wasn't academic, or didn't seem to be until he hit the age of around 13. He told me later that a teacher at the school had said he would never amount to anything in his life. This made him want to achieve academic brilliance.

He started off in the lowest classes for every subject, the ones for the boys who the school know are not going to achieve success—well, academic success, anyway.

He got along well with the other kids, and he still had all his friends there from primary school.

A lot of the time, Jules said he spent lunchtime in the library, as he would get bored with what his friends talked about. I found this rather odd, but Jules had never been one to be into video games or to talk about girls constantly.

His friends were typical boys, but they were all quite nerdy.

I put this down to Jules being very quiet and very arty. Maybe he didn't always fit in with the other boys.

He would mostly stay at home on the weekends, and he would do things like calligraphy and paint and do Lego. He was just a different sort of kid, I thought.

After Jules realised he wanted to get better grades, he asked me to get him a tutor for math's and science. I hired one of the year 12 boys at the school to come and help tutor Jules. After about two months he got into the specialist maths class and had become one of the school's top performing students. I was astounded!

He continued to delight me with his achievements and marks on his tests and assignments. He was so determined. He studied day and night.

I know most parents would say their kids couldn't be bothered doing schoolwork or studying, but Jules was the opposite. I had to tell him not to study so much.

At the end of year 12, he had a 96.7 ATAR score and was accepted to every university in the state. He was also offered scholarships at all these universities. He also received the 'Edmund Rice Award'. This prestigious award is chosen by the students at the school. They all get to vote the one person that they look up to and is willing to help them with anything they need. This was Jules—a beautiful and caring boy who would tutor kids at the high school he attended just so he could help them. He never got paid for it.

He would also come back to the school to do talks to the kids and explain to them how well they could do if they really tried. Just like Jules had done. Starting off at the basic level and achieving one of the highest scores for the year.

When Jules was nine, I got pregnant with my second child. I never thought I would have another, but my biological clock was ticking, and I decided to give it a go. My second pregnancy was easy, and she came right out. I was so excited to have a girl!

She was very different right from the start. I couldn't quite put my finger on it, but she didn't act like other kids. She also screamed a lot but seemed very angry at times too.

My sister-in-law Tess said one day that she was looking after River, and she asked Tess to draw her a picture. She said she wanted Tess to draw her a picture of a horse. When Tess drew it, River looked at it and yelled at her, 'That is not a horse,' and ripped it into bits.

By the time River was eight, I had her assessed, and she was diagnosed with Asperger's. I don't think we use that term anymore, as it all comes under the autism umbrella.

Jules was great with River. Once Jules could drive (that was a long process), he would take her out to the movies and to any friend's outings or anywhere she needed to go. They were close and are still close today. I used to cry to Jules every time a teacher would tell me what she had done at school, and he would say, 'It's okay, Mum. We will work it out.'

My husband worked long hours, so I pretty much oversaw the schooling and household. I still worked throughout these years with my husband, but Jules was always there to lend me a hand if needed.

Jules started university the following year after high school. He talked about a gap year, but I didn't think it was a good idea. I had heard from several parents that some of their kids had started a gap year and then never went back to university. This isn't always the case, but I didn't want Jules to just have a break if he wasn't going to travel or work the whole year.

Jules had always travelled everywhere with us. We did numerous camping trips and trips on the boat. We also did a lot of overseas travels most years. We went to America a couple of times. New Zealand, Japan, Thailand and Phuket and many more places. When Jules was the only child in the family, we would take my good friend Rochelle's son Blake, and he would keep Jules company. Jules was quite a shy kid, so even though he had friends, he was reluctant to ask them to come over or go out, in case they rejected him. Having Blake there was perfect.

Jules was and is still to this day a huge Lego fan. The walls in Julian's bedroom are piled high with Lego.

When we did one of our trips to America, we took Jules and River to Legoland. I have never seen Jules so happy. He practically skipped around the whole of Legoland like he was in another world.

At the end of the day there, he spent every single cent of his money on Lego. This obsession continues to this day.

Jules also did some trips with the school to Italy and to America again. You could say he was very well travelled.

PART ONE

THE GIRLFRIEND

2019

We were on our way back from our girls' trip. My friend Rochelle has a holiday day house that's on the beach at one of the towns down south. A beautiful house with heaps of bedrooms and bathrooms. There were four of us girls this trip, and as usual, we had way too fun to drink and a lot of fun. We try to get down there at least once a year for a good catch up.

We are in Rochelle's car coming home when my phone buzzes. It's Jules wanting to know when I will be home. He wants to go for a walk with me and our dog Blue. Well, it's really Julian's dog. Our last one Muzzle died only after two years of having him. He was only seven, and it was heartbreaking.

Blue was a rescue dog and such a handful that I wanted to give him back after only a week. Jules begged me not too, and he was so upset from Muzzle's death that I had to say, 'Yes, we can keep him.'

I hated to see Julian upset for any reason. I was definitely a mother who could not stand to see her kids unhappy.

Blue has now been with us for three years, and I am slowly seeing the signs that he is getting better behaved with other dogs and with people.

He will never be a social dog, but we can handle him like this.

Jules has walked with me every day in the mornings since he was little. He never missed a day with me unless he was unwell or away travelling.

We were a very close mother and son. We would not only walk together, but we would go out to lunch together. We would go to the movies together (we both loved a good horror flick) and spend hours at Lego exhibitions, train shows and basically anything that Jules wanted to go to.

He wasn't the most social kid, though he did have some close friends. I think he thought if he invited them over, they might say no, and I don't think he was very good at handling rejection.

I sometimes worried that he wasn't very social, but I put it down to the fact that he was a quiet and a bit subdued when it came to socialising. He wasn't one to go out partying at nightclubs by any means. He would prefer to build Lego in his bedroom at home.

He had started badminton with one of his mates at university and played that a couple of times a week. He really enjoyed it and that was a bit of a social outlet for him.

He also did tutor on the side for some students that were doing year 11 and 12. He got paid for this and really enjoyed it. Like I said, he loved helping people.

When I got back from the girls' trip, Jules seemed quite excited to me and go for a walk with Blue. When I was walking with him, he seemed distracted by his phone.

This rarely happened, as he wasn't into any video games, TikTok, social media or anything like that.

He had a profile on Facebook, but one of his friends set it up for him, as he really had no idea. He never posted pictures or videos on there, but I would often tag him in my pictures if we were on holidays.

As Jules kept looking at his phone, I became curious. 'What are you looking at there, love?'

'Oh, nothing much,' Jules said.

'Why do you keep laughing, then?'

'No reason,' came his reply.

I thought, *What's this kid is up to?*

Jules told me the next day that he had a girlfriend. To be honest, I was really shocked. I really thought Jules might be gay. I asked him several times, but he used to give me a firm 'no' every time.

Kevin and I used to joke that he would need a full body condom to have sex with anyone. He couldn't stand germs and refused to eat anything on his plate if it had been touched at all. We both wondered, *How he would go with even kissing a girl?*

I was truly happy for Jules, though. He told me that she was a girl in his chemistry class who was called Sally. She had asked him out. In his words, he told me that she had said that she had better make a move on him, because otherwise, another girl was going to snap him up.

I agreed with Jules on this. He was a good looking, smart and caring boy. What's not to like about him?

The only reason he didn't have a girlfriend, I thought, was because he was so shy.

When he was younger, he did have a crush on a girl in his primary school. They played a lot together, and when they were out, they would always hold hands. It was so cute! Since then, though, I never even saw him look at another girl! I did see a lot of girls look at him, though.

Jules told me that he was inviting Sally over on the Friday and if I could be home later to meet her. I was a little anxious, as I hadn't been in this situation before, but I was excited for him.

Friday came, and I arrived home and went upstairs to meet her.

I have to say, I was quite shocked. I mean I am not one to judge a book by its cover, as they say, but really, what did Jules see in this girl?

She stood about five foot nothing. She had red frizzy hair and not a very welcoming face, to say the least. My first thought was, *Shit, she is batting above her average.*

Then I thought, *Well, who am I to judge?* He must see something in her, otherwise why would he go out with her? She must be very smart and on his wavelength.

Julian was in his third year of chemistry at this stage, and he wanted to do honours and then do a further PhD, hopefully with a scholarship.

He started off doing physics but became bored after about six months, as it was more to do with computer coding. Not really his scene.

He switched to chemistry, which was more hands-on in a lab.

I thought this would be the subject that he studied, as when he was young, he was forever making bombs with his mate Stan. They were handmade ones, and they would make them and then light them up. I was paranoid every time they made one thinking they would blow their hands off.

So, their dating days began.

I started to notice small changes in Julian almost immediately. They were subtle but still there. Jules was still walking with me every morning, but things had started to change. He became more withdrawn from me. I know this is what comes with getting a girlfriend, but it was not in a good way. I really didn't think too much of it, but I did notice a lot of things he had started to criticise about our home and how in a lot of ways it was not up to standard.

I mean, small things like, 'Why don't we have better cookware? Sally's parents have the top of the range frying pans, and you just buy these crap ones.' And 'Why is the pool so small? Sally's house has a big infinity pool that overlooks the bushes. We can see kangaroos and birds and everything from her backyard.'

'Well, I am sorry we don't live out in the bush,' I would sarcastically say to Jules. 'We have always lived in the city, and you have always liked living here.'

I mean, our house is certainly big and by any standards very liveable, even if the pool is a little small and even if I don't buy the best frypans around. I mean, who really cares about this shit, anyway? These were first-world problems, and Jules had never bothered about anything like that before.

'Well, I think I would prefer to live out in the bush,' Jules said. 'I really don't think I like living in this area.'

'That's the first I have heard of that,' I said to him. 'You said you love living here.'

'Not anymore,' he said and sauntered off to his room.

How unappreciative, I thought. I knew it was she instigating all of this, but I could not believe how easily Jules was brainwashed by her.

He was spending a lot of time at her house now. She lived about an hour away from us, so it was a good drive for Jules to get there. Sometimes, he would just go straight from university to her house and wouldn't come home for a couple of days.

I thought this was fine, as he was in love.

Not long after they had started seeing each other, Julian came home and announced he was gluten intolerant.

'That's absurd!' I said 'You've never had that problem in your whole life.'

'It can happen at any time in your life,' he said, 'and it has happened to me now.'

What a load of crap, I thought. She is really getting to him. Gluten intolerant my ass!

I knew Sally was gluten intolerant, along with a huge list of other things that were a problem. Things like she couldn't put a toothbrush in her mouth because she couldn't stand the bristles and the fact that she seemed to have a period every two weeks and with that came a whole lot of pain and misery. She constantly stated that she had a headache, and Julian would curse me if he went to the cupboard and we didn't have any Panadol in it. *She sounds like a drama queen*, I thought. A total narcissistic bitch!

Rock climbing had become Julian's new preferred sport. Obviously, it was because it was her sport. He continued to play badminton occasionally, but he now did rock climbing with her at least three times a week.

It seemed that everything that was her hobby was now his hobby too.

She is slowly but surely pulling him away from his friends and probably from us too.

He now spent his weekends at her parent's house. Apparently, every Saturday night, they would all play a family board game, and on Sunday, they would both spend time with Sally's friends and play Dungeons and Dragons. How boring is that I thought? What sort of 20-something-year-olds spend their lives doing boring shit like that? When I was their age, I was out drinking and partying, not sitting at a table playing a boring game like that on the weekend.

Jules came home one day and told me that we should do that as a family and that we were not a close family, unlike Sally's family, who were extremely close apparently.

'What do you mean by that?' I shouted. 'Not close? You have been everywhere around the world with us. You have been on every camping trip with us until you were 20. You have built a car with your dad over the past eight years as a project. You used to walk with me every morning with the dog. What the hell?' I screamed at him. 'You think that by playing a board game every Saturday afternoon will make us a close family? What a load of shit! That is never going to happen!'

He sulked and walked off. I knew it was her talking and not Jules. She was part of this new Jules that I no longer knew. He did everything that she wanted.

Sally didn't like his group of friends, so she refused to see them, so Jules hardly saw them anymore either.

This was very sad, as Jules had had this group of friends since he was in kindergarten.

What was even more sad was that I could see all this unfolding before my eyes, but it was just the tip of the iceberg. I didn't know I was about to hit it head on.

I was starting to dislike her more and more. It was like she was turning him against me. The more time she spent with him, the more distant he became. It wasn't like I was trying to keep him all for myself and be selfish. I knew that he was going to spend a lot more time with his girlfriend than with me, but it just wasn't how I pictured it.

Jules has stopped walking the dog with me completely now. He doesn't have much to do with any of his family anymore. One time, I asked him if he could drop off some food with me to the local homeless centre, and he blatantly replied, 'I don't have time for that. I am meant to be at Sally's in an hour.'

I would ask him to pick up something for me from the shop on the way home. 'I haven't got time,' would be his reply.

This was very sad and so unlike Jules. He would have done that no problem before. He would have said, 'Yeah, no worries, Mum. I am running late, but I will nip into the shop and grab it for you on the way back.' He would have also made time to help other people in need as that was who he was. He had helped with so many causes in his life. He did things like the 'fun run' with me every year for charity. He had helped several times with the black dog on a lead for men's mental health and had also helped me with dropping off food for the homeless people on numerous occasions amongst other things.

I couldn't even get him to help me with anything around the house. Kevin worked long hours, so Jules was always my go-to person to help me with any small things that needed doing. Now, he was too busy to help me with anything.

The only thing now that seemed important to him was doing what she wanted him to do. It was like he was her dog on a lead, her puppet to control the strings to make Jules do everything that he was told to do. It was so bizarre. I thought it would be the other way around, considering her personality and her lack of anything that you would class as attractive.

Not long after that, Jules came home and announced that he was asexual. *What the fuck is that?* I thought.

Jules then began to explain that he has never had any sexual desires of any kind. I am quite old school, so again, I thought, *How the fuck does that happen? No sexual desire?* I have been having sexual desire since I was about 16. There was no way I would have ever gone through life thinking I was never going to have sex. *That is just ridiculous! It's just so unnatural,* I thought.

I made this known to Jules and told him that what he is saying is just ridiculous! Now, I am certain that it probably can be a thing, but I knew he was only saying that because she was like that.

I told Kevin about this later when he got home from work, and he said the same thing. 'What the fuck does that mean?' and then he added she that she probably doesn't have a fanny.

'Is that a thing?' I said to Kevin, looking at him like he had a great deal of knowledge on the subject.

'Well, she is a pretty small person, so maybe there's no opening down there.' He liked to lighten the mood a lot and does say a lot of funny things like that.

We had a bit of a laugh about it, as I thought to myself that it won't stay like that. They are just both virgins who fear doing it for the first time. That's all it is.

Still, I was very worried. Who is this person in my house? This is not my Jules. He is a stranger of his former self that stands before me. An imposter! He is telling me these things because she is saying them. It's like he has no mind of his own anymore. He is totally and utterly brainwashed! How can a kid who is so intelligent let this bitch rule his mind and his life.

He has taken up rock climbing because she does it. He is now gluten intolerant because she is. He has decided he is now asexual because she is.

All these things he is doing are because she is telling him that's what he is.

He is starting to spend more and more time at her house too. I hardly see him, anymore. Not that I am this overprotective mother that needs her son with her all the time, but we used to be so close.

I feel like she is totally controlling him, and I can't do anything about it.

He also has become very distant towards his sister River. This is very unlike Julian. One day, he came downstairs and asked me why River was like that.

'Like what?' I replied.

'Like, she says weird shit all the time.' It was almost as if he was embarrassed of her.

'She has the tism,' I said. Tism was a word that we made up for her. It was a shortened version of autism. Whenever she would go somewhere or do something, she would say, 'Shall I tell them about the tism?'

It was an ongoing joke in our house. River was quirky, intelligent and definitely very different, but she would still laugh at herself. At times, she could be very dark, but she was very witty and funny. Being on the spectrum as she was, it was hard for her to control what she said at times. She would say weird stuff like, 'I want to be a table when I grow up,' or 'why can't I be a fish?'

I was stunned by what Jules was saying to me. How could he be embarrassed of his little sister? He used to go to the movies with her and take her to lunch with him and to the shop with her. When she got a bit older, he would take her to conventions in the city. I thought they were always so close, but now, he was pushing her away.

It's her, I thought. She doesn't like River. She hardly speaks to Kevin or me, and now, she doesn't want to speak to River either.

It was always quite awkward in my house when she was here.

They were starting to share a car together, as they were always together anyway. They had separate cars, but because they went to university together and were now in each other's pockets constantly, they decided it would be better to use just the one car.

This was convenient for them, I guess, but I would never know if she was at our house then.

I would come home from work and scream 'hello' as I walked into the house. River would never hear me, as she always had her headphones on in her room, so that was to be expected. There were no other voices, so I would assume there was nobody else in the house.

I would walk up the stairs and open Julian's bedroom to put some of his mail in the room, and she would be lying on his bed.

'Oh, I didn't know you were here' I said. 'Hello'

'Hello,' Sally would say.

There was no other conversation. Not a 'How was your day?' or a 'How are you doing?' It was seriously like she couldn't be bothered making conversation with me.

It was so awkward. I felt like I was an imposter in my own home.

I had heard some other of my friends comment on their sons' girlfriends and how rude they were, and I thought, *Well, she is well and truly one of those girls*. Maybe it will change but I really couldn't see that happening in the foreseeable future. It probably will never happen. She just doesn't like us.

It wasn't just that, though. She would now sleep over at night and would get up in the morning and walk past me in the kitchen and not even say 'Good morning.' I couldn't get over this amount of rudeness. It was if we didn't exist in our own home.

I would be cooking in the kitchen, and she would come downstairs, even if Julian wasn't home, and start making cakes or something. Gluten free, of course.

I felt like I was an alien in my own home. She made me feel so uncomfortable. I felt like screaming at her 'Will you just fuck off out of my house!' If I did that, Jules would probably never talk to me again.

Then, early 2020, COVID hit, and they both decided to isolate at our house. This was difficult, to say the least. *Why can't they go to her house?* I thought. *They are there all the time, anyway.*

Even when they were isolating, I was thinking, *It's not much different to your real life.* All they seemed to do these days was to sit upstairs in Julian's room and watch anime series all day. Even if it was nice weather, they still sat inside and watched TV all day.

At least watch something decent, I thought. Jules and I used to watch horror flicks and crime series and different things like that. Now all they watched was this crap. Obviously because she liked it.

I could imagine Jules coming downstairs and saying, 'Hey, Mum, do you want to watch that new horror flick on TV?' That was the old Jules. He was now replaced by the brainwashed version.

As the relationship continued, the things they used to do together got less and less. The rock-climbing adventures were seldom now. Sometimes, they could do university from home so then they never had to leave the house. It seemed like an unhealthy relationship to me.

'Go out and get some sunshine,' I'd say.

'Sally's got a headache,' Jules would say, or 'Sally has period pain.' *Fuck, she is a pain in the ass*, I thought. *It is always about her, and she is always whining!*

Sometimes, Jules would just go for a walk on his own. If he went to see his friends, which he did do occasionally but less and less these days, then he would just go by himself. She would stay at home, even if she was at our house. I found this annoying, as I thought, *Jules is always socialising with your friends, yet you can't make any effort with his*. It didn't seem very fair to me, but Julian just accepted this. He continued to see her friends on a regular basis, and they became more of 'his friends group' as such.

We were over on our boat one day at our favourite little island getaway when I got a phone call from Julian. We would try to get over there at least a few times a year. It is such a beautiful little island where you can snorkel and swim and catch heaps of fish and crayfish.

Both the kids used to come when they were younger. Jules kept coming with us right up until he was 18 or even older.

'You will never guess who Sally was friends with at school?' He says.

'Who?'

'Gemma,' he says.

'No way! What a weird coincidence!'

'Yeah,' he says. 'She was friends with her for a few years when they were in high school.'

Gemma was the girl that Jules used to play with in primary school. She was a lovely girl, but the same couldn't be said for the mother.

Jules had, before Sally, met up with her a couple of times for a coffee, and I think he thought that they might get together at some point.

I thought this could probably work at the time, but I still had an inkling that he might be gay. Well, I guess he couldn't be if he liked Gemma.

The only reason I wouldn't want this relationship to happen, I thought, was the fact that Gemma's mother was toxic. Well, in my opinion she was.

I had been very good friends with her when the kids were at primary school together. It was because the kids were quite close that we became good friends.

Now that I am not friends with her anymore, I can now see how toxic she was.

Melissa was her name. She was one of these mothers who thought they were better than anyone else. She was quite well off but not through her own hard work. It was because her parents were literally loaded.

She would always have the best handbag, the best shoes, the best car, pretty much the best everything!

There were other mothers at the school who formed her little group, and I was one of them.

I was never a gossipy or a 'give a fuck' sort of girl. I wasn't a name dropper or a person who knows the latest fashion labels. I always looked after myself by going to the hairdresser every four weeks, going to the beautician, getting my nails done and going to the gym on most days, but I was not a 'Hey look at what bag I've got' sort of person.

Don't get me wrong, I do like my luxuries, especially as I have gotten older, but I have never been that person who compares themselves to other people. She was one of those people, and so were all her friends. Well, there were a couple of exceptions, but most of them were just bitches!

When we would meet for coffee or maybe lunch, they would bitch about the other parents and how the kids were dumb or which reading class they were in. If they were in the special reading class, then they would laugh about it. The special reading class was for the kids who couldn't read very well for their age. Of course, none of their kids were in this class.

They would talk about how clever their kids were and what sport they were good at and everything that was wrong with the other kids in the classroom.

One of the mothers, Trish, was a right cow. I never really liked her at all but would just go along with it because she was part of the group. She would say how amazing her older kids were and how clever they were and how well her daughter in the class was doing. I would think to myself, *Well, your daughter and your other two sons might be doing well, but you're still an ugly, fat bitch, and that isn't ever going to change*, but I would never say anything. I knew deep down that she was an ugly person on the inside as well as the outside and that she was probably trying to make up for her own lack of self-esteem by bagging other parents and kids. I would just let her rant about everyone else's kids and how stupid they are, all the time thinking I don't belong with this group of people.

I never felt good about hanging out with those mothers, and now that I think about it, I see that the other parents at the school might have thought I was one of these gossipy, nasty mothers who bagged all their kids. I was not like this at all, but it wasn't until I was out of that cliquey group that I realised how toxic it was.

It had all come to a head when Melissa had Jules over and took her two daughters and him out to get an ice cream in her brand-new car, which had leather seats, of course.

One of the kids had apparently written the name Gemma on the back of the passenger seat while she was driving the car. When she told me about it, she said she didn't know which of the kids it was, but she had made them all write their names on a piece of paper, and it looked like Julian's writing. How she could know this when the writing could have been different if they were moving, I have no idea.

That did it for me! I couldn't deal with her or her fucked up friends anymore. I stopped seeing all of them, and shit, did they make my life hell at school!

None of them would talk to me at all! There was one nice lady in the group who still spoke to me, but other than that, they all ignored me.

When I had River, I couldn't bring myself to be friends with any of the mothers at the school, as I was paranoid that this might happen all over again! I had become totally paranoid about getting into another toxic group like that.

Anyway, it turned out that Jules and Sally decided to meet up with Gemma for a drink one day. I don't think any-thing really came out of it. I think Gemma was just doing the right thing by meeting up with them, and I don't think Jules saw much of her again until a couple of years later.

Things got progressively worse with Jules.

He had now taken to almost kicking the dog outside if it so much even touched Sally. That was another thing. Apparently, she was allergic to animals, so Blue had to be put outside every time she was there. That was not okay with me, as Blue had always been an inside dog. He used to sleep on Julian's bed with him before the bitch came into the picture. I mean, Blue was predominantly Julian's dog in the first place, and now he was acting like a complete arsehole to him. I was so upset that he was acting like this towards his own dog. It was so mean and so upsetting for me.

Jules then came out and told me one day that he didn't want to help with River anymore. He said he had helped enough and that I was expecting too much from him.

I was so angry with this comment. My reply was, 'Then fucking don't! You don't have to help me with her ever again,' I said, with venom in my voice.

I mean, I always thought he would be there to help me with her, but it wasn't like I needed him there. River was quite independent, and she could do most things on her own. It might be that she just needed a lift to school or maybe to a kid's party or something like that. This was when Jules would help me with her. Sometimes, he would even offer. For him to say this just threw me! It was so unlike him.

One day on a Friday when I came home from work, Jules was sitting at the kitchen bench by himself.

'Hey honey, what's up?' I asked.

His reply was, 'I think I need professional help, Mum.'

'What? Why?' came my reply. I was gobsmacked to say the least.

River had always needed professional help because of her autism. She saw numerous professionals psychologists, counsellors, paediatricians, just to name a few.

He was the perfect boy. He was intelligent, loving and caring and didn't seem to have any mental challenges. So why now? Why did he need to see a professional? What the hell had she done to him?

It all pointed to her again. He had been on a downhill slide since meeting her, and now this.

'Okay, love,' I said calmly. 'I will see if I can find a psychologist for you to see on Monday.' I was going out to the pub that night to watch a footy game. I sat at the pub and watched the football. I could not concentrate on the game. All I could think about was Jules.

'I don't understand it,' I say to my sister-in-law Tess the next day as we are walking with Blue. 'I don't know what could possibly be wrong with him.'

She shakes her head saying she has no idea either. 'He has never said that anything is wrong with him. I mean, I know he is sort of OCD and a bit of a perfectionist with certain things, but does he really need to seek professional advice?' I stammer to her.

Tess said she doesn't have any idea what could be wrong with him.

On Monday, I try to find Julian a psychologist. I mean, he is 20 years old now and classed as an adult, so I obviously can't sit in on what he says to them, and I am not sure I even want to. I really don't think I can deal with two kids who are like this—two kids who both need professional help. One maybe but two? I feel anxious as to what this could be all about.

Her, I think again. *This is all about her! She is ruining him. She is fucking him up in the head! He was relatively normal until he met her, and now, he needs professional help.*

I eventually found Jules a local place that specialises in mental health for adolescents. They help kids of the ages 15–24. They tell me there is at least a six-week wait list. *How many fucked up teenagers are there*, I think?

I don't remember any one of my friends ever seeking professional help. In fact, I don't remember any people that were in my school that needed professional help.

Is this a good or bad thing that now that hundreds and thousands of teenagers need professional help? Will it help them from something as awful as suicide, or is it just the new normal? Why is there such a long waiting list?

I mean, River has always had access to it, but she is autistic. *What is Julian's problem?* I think. *What could possibly be wrong with him? I have given him everything. I have given both of my kids everything. Yet, here I am with two kids needing therapy.*

Julian takes it upon himself to ring the place within two weeks. He tells them he is desperate for help, and they find him a place to see the psychologist the following Friday.

Thank goodness, I think. Now he can get help and get better. Little did I realise how dire the situation would become.

He starts seeing the psychologist on a regular basis. Just about every week. I never ask him what he talks to him about, but I assume it is helping him, and that's all that matters. Hopefully in a few months, he will be back to how he was before.

I don't know if this will be the case if he keeps seeing Sally, though. I mean, she is the one who has caused this in the first place. If she hadn't met him, then he wouldn't need professional help. He would have just been going through his university degree and playing badminton with his friends and being the loving and helpful Julian that he always was.

I wished it were that simple…

Things are starting to deteriorate with Jules now, and it's happening way too quickly.

He is starting to get very angry with me and with Kevin. He is also getting angrier with River if she tries to speak to him at all. On top of that, it is almost like he hates the dog. 'Fuck off, Blue!' he would yell if the dog even came close to him.

He does the same with River. She pops her head into his bedroom to ask him if he's alright. 'Leave me alone!' he shouts at her and slams the door.

I plead with him, 'What's going on, Jules?'

I just don't understand, and I am getting worried sick constantly now. It is affecting my health. I feel sick every day worrying what is wrong with him.

He seems to be getting worse, not better, and he is losing weight. A lot of weight.

He tells me it's to do with the fact that he has a gluten-free diet.

'Well, then don't have a gluten-free diet,' I practically plead with him. 'Just eat whatever you used to eat. You used to eat anything and drink diary and have muffins every day, and now this?' I am screaming at him now. I am at a complete loss as to what is happening here.

'I have to, Mum!' He shouts at me. 'Gluten doesn't agree with me.'

'That's fucken bullshit, and you know it! You just don't eat it because she doesn't!'

He tells me to leave him alone and slams the bedroom door on me.

Sally is coming over more and more now and trying to help Jules with his depression. It is kind of a bittersweet situation, because I hate her and can't stand the sight of her, but on the other hand, I want her there so she can be with Jules so I don't have to be there all the time.

I am so scared that he is going to do something to himself. I picture the worst-case scenario all the time— that I might pop my head in his room one day and he has committed suicide; that I come in and he has overdosed or hung himself.

I constantly check his bank account, which I can see on my phone. I check to see if he has been out and has paid for something online. Then I will know that he is out somewhere and he is okay.

This plagues me constantly, and it is getting hard for me to concentrate at work or to not think about what is going on with him all the time.

I have taken to riding my bike. I go for a couple of hours at a time and listen to audiobooks just so I don't have to be constantly around this depressed boy! This happened so quickly, and it's making my head spin. He is slowly getting more and more depressed, and it is slowly making me more and more anxious about how to fix the situation or whether it can be fixed.

I must do this every day to keep sane, I tell myself, and I truly believe I do. I am still going to work, but because I have other things there to occupy my mind, it stops me thinking about this situation all the time. It stops me thinking, *Why the fuck Jules would do this to me? How could he be depressed? He has a loving family. He has friends. He is smart. He has an unimaginable amount of Lego in his room, and he has travelled all over the world with us. What the hell is his problem?*

Sally texts me from her phone. 'Julian's fainted,' she says.

I ring immediately. 'Oh my god. Is he okay?'

'He's fine,' she says, but I am not convinced.

'Has he eaten today?'

'I think he might have?'

'Can you get him on the phone please?'

Jules sounds groggy. 'It's okay, Mum. I'm fine'

'You are clearly not fine, Jules. You need to eat. You need to eat now! You have never fainted before in your life, and it's because you are not eating! You look like you're anorexic, for God's sake!' I wail down the phone. 'Fucking eat something!'

I get off the phone and slump on the couch. I just don't understand what's going on with Jules. I mean, I thought it would be so nice for him to have a girlfriend, and now this is what happens. This is fucked! This is so fucked!

I started to read every article I can find on mental health issues with adolescents and how I could help with it. I don't know how to help, though, if I don't know what the hell is going on in that head of his.

With his weight plummeting drastically, I am starting to get friends and family making comments to me. I mean, he has probably lost around 25 kilos in the space of a few months, and he looks like he is sick.

My neighbour across the road comes over one day when I am getting out of my car. 'Is Julian okay?' He says, 'I don't want to be nosy or anything, but he looks really sick.'

Mick looks worried, and I am too.

'No, he's okay,' I lie. 'He has just lost a lot of weight because he is doing a lot of rock climbing.'

I feel tears start to spring into my eyes.

I really can't believe this is happening to Jules and to us. He has only been with Sally for less than a year, and he is now at the lowest point I have ever seen him in his life.

'Oh, okay then,' Mick says. 'I was just really worried that he might have cancer or something like that. Marcy was really worried too.'

Marcy is Mick's wife.

That is how bad he looked. He had deteriorated so quickly. Like a walking skeleton.

I am at work one day, and he comes in and sits down at my desk. I ask him if he's okay, and he hands me a note that has the name of an antidepressant on it and what milligram should be taken.

I have never been fond of myself or anyone in my family taking these, as I believed people can become addicted to them.

One of my friends a long time ago had been on them, and then she had told me two weeks before she committed suicide that she had come off them. It was so tragic. She left behind two children and an ex-husband, and they had no idea. This has stuck with me ever since, and I have always been wary of anyone who I love taking them.

I look at him and say, 'No, Jules, you don't need these. You just need to get back on your feet again.'

'I do need these, Mum. I am not getting any better, and the doctor says it would be for the best.'

'You might get addicted to them,' I say. 'Some people are on these prescriptions drugs, and then they never get off them. Or worse still, they get off them and then commit suicide.

'That's not the case,' he says. 'But I really need these, Mum. I think I need them to survive.'

I feel sick. I can't concentrate. All I can think about is Jules. How sick he is and how thin he is and how this has happened to him.

Not long after, Julian told me he had started the antidepressants. He was prescribed fluvoxamine, and he started off on 200 mg. This was quite a high dosage, but he needed to get better.

At this stage, I thought this might be a good thing for him. I could not see any light at the end of the tunnel for him improving, and I thought this might be the only solution.

He was seeing a psychiatrist at this stage for the medication. Not only was Jules on the antidepressants but he also prescribed him quetiapine. This is an antipsychotic drug.

It is usually prescribed for people who have a schizoaffective disorder and psychotic episodes. *But he doesn't have these symptoms*, I thought. It was only because he was with her that he might have these symptoms.

Only a handful of my friends and some family members knew about this, as I didn't want to alarm anyone as to how bad the situation was.

This was around July 2020. I thought then that it was just a phase he was going through. I mean, so many young adults have problems these days, and they are all going on medication. I guess it's just the new norm.

Julian continued his studies at university. He was well into his third year of chemistry and was hoping to do chemistry honours in 2021.

Things did not get better. In fact, they got progressively worse from here.

One day, I get home and find Julian drinking by himself. That is weird for Jules, as he has never been much of a drinker. Maybe an occasional one or two if he's out, but never would he drink alone. Unlike me, who can have a drink alone anytime. In fact, most nights, at least two glasses of wine. More on weekends or when I go out.

That night, I had gone to bed and Kevin wakes me up and tells me Sally came and picked Jules up and he went to her house around 11 pm. Even worse, he was going to drive himself there. She lives about an hour away from where we live.

Kevin tells me Jules is in a terrible state and that he had to beg Jules to phone him to let us know he was okay. I didn't sleep hardly at all that night.

I hadn't heard from Jules the following morning, and I was beside myself, to say the least. I went walking with Blue and met up with my sister-in-law Tess.

As soon as I saw her, I burst into tears. She knew the dramas I was having with Julian, and she was there to listen to me. She listened as I cried and told her I didn't know what I could do to help him. Neither did she, so all she could do was to let me talk.

When I saw Julian later on that day, he told me that Sally had to take him to the hospital. 'What the hell?' I screamed. 'Why did you need to go to the hospital?'

'Because I wanted to commit suicide,' he said blank faced.

I started to sob and scream and tell him how he was making my life miserable. 'How could you do this to me? All I have ever wanted you to be is happy. Why the fuck can't you be happy?'

I had never argued with Jules in my life. Sure, we had the occasional bickering session but never a full-blown argument.

I start sobbing hysterically. I start smashing glasses and kicking furniture and yelling at the top of my lungs. I scream to whoever can hear me, 'Why are you doing this to me? I already have a kid who is autistic, and now my son wants to die? You have given me two kids who are mentally challenged. What the hell did I do to deserve this?'

I keep screaming and crying and kicking furniture until eventually, I lie on the floor in the kitchen and just sob.

I can hear Julian upstairs. He is kicking his bedroom door in. Even today, when I look at that door and the hole in it, I remember how bad I was.

It is approaching Julian's 21st birthday, and for months prior, I had been planning a big party at our house to celebrate.

Julian is not doing any better, though. Lately, I feel like I must be available 24/7. He is still trying to go to university most days, but I am getting to the point where I don't even want him to drive. I am so scared that he will have an accident.

He will call me at work because he is not feeling well, and I feel like I must come home. I talk to him and take him for a walk, but he is in another world. He just walks with his head down, looking like a zombie, while I keep talking and try to lift his spirits. This is such hard work, and I am completely exhausted from it.

Sally is still coming over, but now, he is getting angry with her. It's like he doesn't want her to be there. The only reason I want her there is so that I don't have to keep coming home all the time to try and console him.

He has started taking quetiapine tablets on top of the antidepressants. These tablets make him delirious. One time, he took one, and it made him fall over in the bathroom. He was so scared that he knocked his front tooth out. I told him to only take them when he was going to lie down and not in the day. I was so scared that he was going to fall down the stairs or hurt himself.

I was now continually getting texts from Sally saying he wasn't too good today or he needed to come home and if I would be there to talk to him.

These texts came at least every couple of days.

I decided to see a counsellor myself, as I felt that I was no longer coping. She was useless.

I made an appointment and turned up a little early, as I thought there might be a waiting room. When I arrived, she then told me that I shouldn't arrive early, as she might be with someone else. How the hell was I to know it was a private house? It didn't mention that on the website.

I literally had no energy to argue. I just started crying from the moment I got there until the moment I left. She told me all the useless information that I already knew. I can't control his life and I need to look after myself. *That's fucking obvious*, I thought. She then told me to do some facial exercises that might help me calm down. *As if that's going to make me calm*, I thought. What a load of crap. I could have paid myself to give me that information.

She sent me away with a sheet that had all the facial exercises for me to do. I threw it in the bin the moment I left and never went back to her.

When I walked outside, I had a message from Sally. She said Julian was bad and he couldn't cope at university. *How is he even doing university?* I thought. I can't even get on with everyday life, let alone study something as difficult as chemistry.

I came home to find Julian on his bed crying. 'What's wrong?' This must be the thousandth time I have asked him this in the past few months.

'I feel bad. I am having all these intrusive thoughts.'

What the hell are intrusive thoughts? I gave him a quetiapine, and he fell asleep.

Sally came over to be with him. *Fucking bitch*, I thought. *You are the one that has caused all this, and you sit with him pretending to help.*

The next day, she is still here with him.

I can hear him sobbing. *How much longer can I deal with this*? I think.

Kevin hasn't gone to work yet. He comes into Julian's room with me.

Again, I ask him 'What's wrong?'

'I don't want to be here. I don't want to live like this.'

'Like what? You have everything. You have a loving family. You have an education. You are smart and beautiful.'

'I'm not fucking beautiful!' he screams at me. 'I hate myself.'

Kevin looks stunned. He is at a loss for words. He just looks at me. He has no idea how to fix this, and neither did I.

I call the psychiatrist. 'He is busy,' the receptionist tells me.

'Please,' I beg her. 'This is an emergency.' I am crying as I speak. I have no energy left. I am a complete wreck.

She manages to get him in, and I drive him to the ward. It is labelled 'Mental Health Ward'. *God help me*, I think. *How did it get to this?*

I walk Julian to the door. He is all skin and bone. His long hair hangs over his face, and he has his sunglasses on. He has a long coat covering his scrawny body, even though it is warm. He looks like a drug addict.

As I walk him in, I think that the only solution now is to have him hospitalised. They might need to feed him through a drip and keep an eye out for him in case he tries to commit suicide.

There can't be any other way.

We walk into reception, and I tell the receptionist his name. I can hardly get it out, as my voice is filled with emotion.

I look across at Jules and don't recognise my own child. *How did we get here?* I think again.

We go into the psychiatrist's office and sit down.

'Well?' he speaks directly at Julian 'What's the matter?'

Julian doesn't answer. He just hangs his head down with his hair hanging over his eyes. His sunglasses remain on his face.

'Julian?'

'Yes?'

'What is the problem?' I am sure the psychiatrist must deal with hundreds of patients a week, and this is just another one of them. But it's not, I think. This is 'My Jules'. This is my child.

I start to answer him. I say that Julian doesn't want to be here and doesn't want to be like this.

'Like what, Julian? What don't you want to be like?'

'I don't know.'

'What do you mean you don't know? Are you taking the antidepressants?'

'Yes.'

'What about the quetiapine?' Have you been taking those when you feel bad?'

'Yes.'

'Julian, take your sunglasses off please.'

He takes them off. I don't recognise this boy who sits before me. His face is sunken. His eyes are red from crying. He looks like a zombie.

'Look, Julian. You need to take one of those tablets before the fire is at a ten. When you feel like the fire is about to take hold of you, you take one. It should only be no more than a five at that stage. Once it reaches a ten, it's too late. Do you understand what I am saying to you?'

'Yes.' Jules shrugs with his head still hanging down.

'Okay, then we have that straight. We might have to alter the dose of your antidepressants. It might be too high for you.'

He scribbles something down on a piece of paper for me. 'He needs to adjust his dosage,' he says to me 'We will see how he goes with that.'

'Thank you so much for seeing us,' I say to him. 'I really appreciate your time.'

As we walk out, I look at my child.

He doesn't even look at me.

I want to shake him. I want to yell at him. I want him to see what he is doing to himself. What he is doing to me and to the family. What the fuck is wrong with him?

31

Maybe the dosage was too high, I think. *Yes, that's the problem. The dosage is wrong. If we alter that then Julian will get better.*

I walk out of the ward feeling slightly better, hoping that the lower dosage will fix the problem.

It doesn't

It is a few weeks before Julian's 21st birthday, and I am making all the party arrangements. There are heaps of people coming. Julian's friends, our family, all of Julian's cousins and my friends. In total, there are around 60 people. I have organised it to be at our house.

I have bought cartons of champagne. Heaps of beer and wine. I have organised a caterer for the event as well as a singer to play some music.

Although I planned this months ago, I am not looking forward to it at all. Julian is not feeling much better than he was on the higher dosage.

He keeps telling me about these intrusive thoughts that he has.

'What do they mean?' I ask him. 'Are they like you want to harm someone or something?'

'Maybe'

'Like who? Me?'

'Maybe. Or maybe myself.'

'Why would you want to do that?'

We are walking Blue, and I am once again trying to keep the mood light. I am trying to keep Jules as positive as possible. I am trying to get Jules excited about his birthday party.

'I don't understand you! You keep talking about this crap, and I don't know what you mean by it. Have you talked to your psychologist about these thoughts?'

'Yes, I have.'

'Well, what does he suggest?'

'I can't talk to you about it,' he says.

Oh well, I think. *At least he is talking to somebody about it so that's got to be better than nothing.*

'I wish I had never organised this party.'

'You can always cancel it'

'It's too hard to do that now. It's less than a week away.'

'It doesn't bother me.'

'What is wrong with you?' I shout. 'I have organised this all for you, and now you don't care if I cancel. Where did I go wrong with my parenting? All I have ever wanted to do is to make my kids happy, and you are both just miserable shits! It's all my doing!'

'It's not your fault, Mum. You are a great parent.'

'Then why are you so depressed?' I am in tears now. 'Why can't he just be the old Jules like before? Why does everything have to be this complicated?'

'Maybe one day, I can tell you,' Jules says.

'Why can't you tell me now? What could be so bad that you can't tell me? I just don't understand!'

We keep walking. We don't say much to each other after that.

The day arrives for the party.

It's a beautiful day and just the right temperature so we can have the party outside.

The caterer turns up and arranges all the food on the table.

The acoustic guitar player arrives and sets up near the outside area.

I have got all the alcohol on ice, and everything is perfect.

Everything except for our family, I think.

Sally calls Jules and says she feels sick. Of course, she is sick. Too sick to meet up with Julian's family and friends to celebrate his birthday, the fucking cow. This is so fucking typical of her. She is so selfish!

To be honest, I am glad she isn't coming. She would only spoil it for Jules. Make it hard for him to communicate with his friends. To hang out and be himself. To just have fun for once.

There are about 60 people invited, and they all turn up.

Jules seems to be in a good mood, so I am thankful for that.

The day wears on, and it comes to around the cutting of the cake time.

I bought heaps of little cupcakes and made them all into a 21 sign.

A few people yell out, 'Speech!'

I always have one ready at parties that we organise, but I couldn't bring myself to do one.

At Julian's 18th birthday, I did a two-page poem that had people in fits of laughter.

I stand near the cakes, and I am lost for words.

'Oh well,' I say, 'I guess you're 21 now Jules. Guess it's time for you to move out.'

Everyone just stares at me.

Kevin comes rushing over.

'Well, Jules,' he starts. He is not one for speeches. 'We are so proud of you and everything that you have achieved in your life so far and I am sure you will achieve in your future. You are a kind-hearted and beautiful soul, and we are lucky to be able to call you, our son. So, let's raise our glasses to Jules. Happy 21st.'

Everyone raises their glasses, including myself.

One of Julian's friends Wayne comes over to where we are standing and says he would like to make a speech.

'Julian is an amazing human being,' he says. 'I have known him since kindergarten, and the whole time I have known him, he has been the most polite and helpful person you could imagine. Whenever any of us boys needed help with any of our schoolwork—or anything else for that matter—Jules would always help us. He is the most beautiful person you will ever meet. And smart. He is so fucking smart!'

All his other friends join in with cheers for Jules

This lightens my spirits a bit. *Maybe we will be okay,* I think.

The party rolls on way into the night, and by the end of it, we are all very drunk.

There is a handful of Julian's friends left and Kevin and me.

I have never seen Julian this drunk before. It is quite amusing.

I go to his room where all his friends are gathered, looking after him.

He is vomiting, and they are all there with towels and buckets.

I tell him I am so proud of him. I am happy that he has had a good time.

It turned out to be a great party. Probably because Sally wasn't there.

After the party, things got progressively worse.

Jules is losing more weight and is still in a complete hole.

He says it's because he needs to be light because of the rock climbing, but he looks unwell. He looks so sick.

Everyone is commenting on how much weight he has lost. Not just the family but also my friends and acquaintances. 'What's going on with Jules?' they ask me.

I really don't know what to say to them.

'He is just looking after his body because he does a lot of rock climbing and needs to be a certain weight,' I lie.

I don't know whether they believe me or not, but I don't know what else to say.

I haven't told many people that Jules is on antidepressants. I know a lot of young and older people are on them these days, but people usually ask the question 'Why?'

That is a question I don't have an answer for.

I come home most days now to look after Jules and try and take him for a walk.

He is still attending university, but he is like the walking dead.

We go for a walk with Blue, and I am constantly trying to lift his spirits. He just walks along with his head down. A shell of the boy I used to know.

The lower dose of drugs hasn't seemed to make much difference with him. He still hardly eats and he is still depressed.

'I have told my supervisor I need time off as I am not well. I am really depressed,' he says to me.

'Why, Jules? I just want you to tell me why you feel like this. I just don't understand. I am trying everything to make you feel better, and nothing is working.'

I am in a complete state now. I can't eat properly or sleep properly. I am drinking way too much to cope with this constant fear that Jules is going to kill himself. I am a total wreck!

I drink in the morning before I go to work as well. Not enough to breathe over the limit, but just a shot or two to get me through the day. I know this is bad for me, but I just don't know how to cope with this continuous fear of Jules harming himself.

It is the worst feeling a parent could have. I don't know the underlying reason, and it is just killing me.

It's Kevin's 50th birthday in a couple of weeks.

We had arranged to go overseas for a cruise with a few friends. We were going to go to Europe for a couple of weeks.

This had been arranged early last year before COVID had hit.

Of course, nobody can travel overseas now, and I couldn't be more thankful.

We had arranged with Jules that he would look after River for the two weeks while we were away.

I can't let Jules look after River in the state he is in.

I can't let Jules even look after himself.

I am so relieved that we are not going. Even if we could still travel, there is no way I can leave Jules like this. I wouldn't be able to enjoy myself. I would be constantly thinking about him and what's going on in his head.

It's a fucking nightmare!

Jules is still managing to go to university most days. I really don't know how he can study in such a state.

Most nights if he comes home, he will just go to his room.

A couple of times, River has knocked on his door and asked him if he's okay.

'Leave me the fuck alone,' he yells at her.

I have never seen this side of him. He never raises his voice, ever.

He is like a drug addict who needs another hit.

He is like an anorexic who needs food.

But he is my son, and I love him.

When I hear him talk like this, it makes me want to cry more. Will this depression ever end?

Christmas is fast approaching, and we had planned to take our workers for a long weekend down south for the Christmas break. I don't know if I will be able to go.

I am beside myself worrying over Jules, and I don't think I could relax enough to even slightly enjoy myself.

One day while Jules was at university, I sneak into his room.

I am looking for any clues as to why he is feeling so depressed.

I know he told me that his psychologist had told him to write everything down in a diary.

I know it's wrong, but I started looking for it. I am hoping that it might shed some light on why Jules is feeling so depressed.

I searched all his cupboards and under all the Lego models. There are Lego models everywhere. I think back to a time when that's all Jules cared about. Building his Lego models. It was the most exciting part of his life.

A long, long time ago. Before he was sick. Before he met that bitch Sally.

I found a drawer that had a lot of art supplies in it. Pencils and brushes and small canvases.

Under one of the canvases is a small book.

His diary.

I know that it is wrong as I am opening it, but I can't help myself. I need to know why he is feeling like this.

I open it to the first page. The last entry that was written.

29th October

I don't want to be here. I don't fit in with anyone. Not my mates, not my colleagues, and probably not even my family.

I don't know why I feel like this but sometimes I wish I was never born.

I just don't know who I am supposed to be.

I can hardly get out of bed in the morning. I can barely function.

I feel like a lost soul that has no cause.

Today I managed to get to Uni, but I don't feel like I belong there either.

I don't know whether these drugs are working or not.

I feel so lost and I feel like I don't want to live anymore.

I shut the diary.

I am in hysterics.

I go and lie on my bed and cry so much that my tears have left marks streaming down my face.

I can't stop. The sick feeling in my stomach is so bad that it is painful.

What was I hoping to find in that book? Some sense of hope that Jules might be getting better.

He is not getting better at all.

He is getting worse. This might never end. This might go on like this for the rest of his life.

How will he cope? How will I cope?

I texted Kevin.

'I can't come to work today,' I type through the tears. 'I just read Jules's diary.'

He phones me.

'What did you do that for?'

'I thought it might enlighten me on why Jules is feeling so down. It's awful, Kevin. He doesn't want to live!' I scream 'Why doesn't he want to live? What the fuck is going on with him?'

'I'm coming home,' he says calmly.

'Okay,' I manage to say.

When Kevin gets home, I am in an absolute state and crying so much that my eyes hurt.

He comes and hugs me. 'What were you thinking looking at Julian's diary?' he asks me.

'I thought maybe I could make some sense of all this. I mean, why is he like this?' I question him. 'He was fine until he met that witch Sally. She has done this to him. She has made him into this person that we don't even know anymore.' I am sobbing now.

'You don't know that,' he says. 'It might be something else that has triggered this.'

'Like what? The only change that has happened in the last six months is that he met her.'

'But you don't know if it's Sally who has done that. Remember, this is the first girlfriend Jules has ever had. It might be affecting his moods.'

'Like this?' I yell 'Like to the point where he wants to kill himself?'

'Look, I don't know what this is all about, but he will figure it out. In the meantime, don't look at his diary again. You know it's going to make you upset.'

'Okay,' I agree, 'I won't look at it again.'

After Kevin goes back to work, I lie in bed for a very long time. I try to listen to meditational music, but nothing is helping at all. All I can think about were those words written in Julian's diary.

When Jules arrives home later that day, he asks me if I am okay.

I tell him I am fine and that I just feel a little sick today.

He doesn't believe me but lets it go.

I never told him that I looked at his diary. I know I should not have delved into his personal life, but I wanted answers.

The answers I found were not the ones I wanted.

It makes me angry to think that he feels like this. It's almost selfish, I think. He has everything. Why is he making my life hell? Why the hell can't he tell me what is going on here?

I don't look at his diary again. Things don't get any better, though.

Sally is still coming over and staying some nights, but most of the time, it's me Jules wants to help him get through the day.

Every day is a struggle for both of us.

This depression is like a parasite that is eating him from the inside out. It is tormenting his brain and killing his body. He is like a walking zombie.

He has no will to live, and I can't help him.

It is now November, and as my birthday approaches, things continue to spiral downwards. Jules is a complete skeleton who won't eat or barely goes out unless he has to go to university.

I can't see an end to his depression.

I keep asking him, 'What is going on, Jules? How are you so depressed? You used to be fine.'

'I don't know why,' he tells me 'I keep having these intrusive thoughts, and they won't go away.'

'I don't know what that means!' I say to him through tears. 'Why can't you explain this to me?'

'I don't know,' Julian shrugs 'I can't.'

My birthday comes, and Jules tries his best to make me a card and buy me a gift. All I really want now is for him to be happy. I don't care about my birthday. All I have ever wanted is for my kids to be happy, and neither of them are. It is a shit birthday!

Still, I try to go through the motions and play the part of being a happy birthday girl. I try to smile and pretend like there is nothing bad going on in my life.

It is now December, and Christmas is fast approaching. We always have a work get together for our employees, and we usually take a couple of days off and go away down south.

I tell the workers that Jules is going through a really hard time. They all know this already, as I have been going home most afternoons to look after him and take him out.

'I am not sure if I will be able to go,' I tell them.

How is it that my now 21-year-old kid needs me there for him? I mean, it's supposed to get easier as they get older.

Now I feel like I can't leave him in case he has a depressive episode. I mean, River can't look after him.

Sally is sometimes there with him, but that is getting less and less now.

I tell Jules that we are going away for the Christmas party, but I can stay here with him if he wants me to.

'No, Mum. Just go,' He says, 'I will be fine, really!'

'Are you sure, honey? I can stay here with you if you like. It's no problem.'

As we were driving down south, we got a phone call from Jules. I put him on speaker in the car. I am preparing myself for bad news, but surprisingly, Jules sounds upbeat.

'I am feeling much better,' he says.

Kevin and I exchange glances.

'I got great marks at university, so I am doing honours next year. I really think I might get a scholarship.'

'Wow, honey, that's amazing! I am so pleased for you. You have worked so hard for this. You really deserve it!' I am beaming. *Maybe it was to do with university*, I think to

42

myself. All that pressure on these kids today to succeed drives them to insanity.

Jules seems one hundred percent to how he was just a week ago. This is a complete miracle.

We say goodbye and hang up.

I turn to Kevin, 'I can't believe Jules sounds so happy. It's like a weight has lifted from his shoulders. Maybe it was just university that was dragging him down.'

'Sounds like it might have been,' Kevin says 'It is so much pressure on these young kids. Maybe Jules can start to get better now.'

'He will,' I say happily to Kevin. 'We will get the old Jules back.'

I would never have dreamt of what was to come…

PART TWO

THE CONFESSION

MARCH 2021

Jules is now doing his last year of chemistry. He has started honours but hoping to get that scholarship that he wants. Another three years with a scholarship would get him his doctorate in chemistry.

This is something I am considerably worried about, as he is counting on getting it. So is Sally. I am worried about the fact that she might get it and he doesn't. I wonder, *How will his mental health be then? Will we have to go through the same devastation again. Will Jules be able to cope with it? Will I be able to? Will the family survive this for a second time?*

Jules comes home one day from Sally's and asks me about his bank accounts. He asks me if I have access to them. I do, as I put $100 away a week for his allowance. He also does tutor a few students on the side, so he makes some money from that.

He has separate accounts for shares, Lego and everyday spending.

I thought this question was very weird and asked him why he wanted to know.

He tells me that he wants to take control of all his money and for me not to interfere with it. I don't interfere with it at all. I just make the payments into it. I never take any money out of it, as that is his money.

I didn't think much more about this strange question and would never think that this was the start of his confession.

Kevin and I are at a convention down south with River. This is something we go to every year with her, or should I say I do. Kevin just happened to come down with me this year. It's a convention that goes for three days, and all the people there dress up in their costumes. They do things like crafts and drawings, discos and artwork. They also have craft markets for people who want to buy costumes and art.

On the last day before we leave to come home, I get a phone call from Jules.

'Hi, Mum.' He goes through the usual chit chat of how it is going down there and what have we been doing etc.

'I have something to tell you.'

'Okay. What is it?' I can only think that he has got his scholarship early and maybe he is itching to tell me. I feel a bit of excitement to think this might be the case.

'I don't want to tell you over the phone. I want to tell you in person.'

'Just tell me now.' I hate it when people say they want to tell me something and then don't tell you right away.

I can hear Sally in the background giggling.

'What is it, Jules? Just tell me.'

'It's nothing bad,' she also echoes this statement in the background.

Well, if it's nothing bad, then it must be okay, I think. But what can it be?

My mind races as I tell Kevin. 'Maybe he realised he's gay,' Kevin says.

'But he can't be if he likes women. It must be something else, like he got the scholarship, or maybe he is going to a different university that accepts talented students,' I say.

Both of us are baffled as to what it might be.

MONDAY 22 MARCH 2021

The next day, we are on our way home. I ring Jules. He is at Sally's again. He has been staying there most nights and is only home one or two days a week.

He answers the phone. 'Jules, tell me, what it is?'

'No, I will come and see you tomorrow and tell you.'

'I can't wait that long. I need you to come and tell me today.'

'I will check with Sally and see if we can get there today.'

'Why does she need to come? Is she pregnant or something?' This is a rhetorical question, to say the least. I mean, I assume they are both still asexual.

'Okay, Mum. We will come today around 2 pm'

I am satisfied with this answer and wait eagerly for them to rock up.

They both come in and sit at the kitchen bench.

Jules hands me a letter

It reads:

I have something quite big to tell you and I hope you know that the past few months have been very difficult for me. You were

49

most respectful and caring at that time, and I truly hope this doesn't break that.

I want you to know that I have thought about this a lot with others as well as myself and am most certain about its conclusion.

So please don't try and ask, 'Are you sure?' because I am sure.

I hope that in time you can accept, and I really hope that you are not discouraged or disappointed.

This is pretty big, so I am going to stay at Sally's for a while to allow you time to process it.

In that time, I hope you can see that I am still me. I haven't changed because of this. Please don't see me as some other person because I'm not.

I look at Julian confused.

'I'm transgender,' Jules blurts out.

'What?'

They both sit there holding hands and giggling. I want to smash their fucking faces together.

This just can't be right. What does it mean to be transgender?

I mean I have seen transgender people on the TV. Caitlyn Jenner comes to mind. I am sure I have seen some out and about in town, but I don't know for sure if they were transgender or were just expressing their femininity. *What is the difference?* I thought. Anyway, surely people that are transgender would have known all their lives that they were. At least the parents would know, I think.

It wouldn't just come out of the blue like this confession has, surely? Jules has never acted like a girl. She has never wanted to try on one of my dresses or put on my make-up or say that she wished she didn't have a penis. None of this makes sense.

I look over at Sally, who is grinning like she has just won the winning lottery ticket. Fucking bitch!

'Do you still want to be with Jules, then?' I ask her.

'Yes, I love Jules for the person she is.'

Really? You can fall in love with a boy and then they become a girl, and you still love them the same? Am I the only one who is ignorant to this generation?

People who love each other for the person and not the gender they are.

This is mind boggling!

'What about your dad?' I ask Jules 'Have you told him?'

'No, you can tell him.'

What is this? Some sort of ominous game they are playing, just to see how I react?

Jules and Sally get up to leave.

'I will give you some time to get used to this. I am going to Sally's for a while.'

Time to get used to it? What the fuck does that mean? I will never get used to it. You came in to tell me this as a boy, and you have walked out of here as a girl, and I am supposed to get used to it?

I stand out the front and watch them get in the car together and drive off.

This is surreal to say the least.

My son has just come home and told me something that is so devastating, and they drive off laughing.

Jules can't mean this, I think. *He's a girl? How is that possible?*

I walk outside and hang the washing out. I start to cry. Heaving, guttural sobs that won't stop. This can't be happening to me. It just can't. I sit out the back on the concrete floor under the clothesline and sob. For a very, very long time.

When I finally got myself together, I ring Kevin to tell him. He starts laughing.

'No he's not!' he snorts. 'Maybe Jules is confused. Maybe he just likes to wear women's clothes, so he thinks he's transgender.'

'Well, Jules sounded pretty sure about it.'

'Look, there is no way that Jules is transgender!' Kevin says. 'We would have known!'

He's right, I think. Jules is confused, that's all.

I go to Bunnings. On the way there, I ring my girlfriend, Rochelle.

I meet her every Friday for breakfast before work. We only ever text each other. We never ring each other unless there is something wrong.

She answers the phone. She is at work. 'What's the matter?'

She knows something must be very wrong for me to call her.

I tell her what Jules has just told me.

I question her, 'Did you ever think Jules was transgender?'

Of course, she didn't. Why was I even asking her that question?

She has no answers for me. She has no advice for me. She is as shocked as I am.

'I don't know what to say,' Rochelle says to me. 'I mean, Jules has never shown any signs of being transgender, right? Maybe Jules just thinks that they are. I mean, all this depression started when Jules met Sally. Maybe she has something to do with all this?'

'Exactly!' I say. 'She is the common denominator here. Ever since Jules met her, it has all been downhill.'

I tell myself that it is all to do with Sally. She has convinced Jules that they are transgender.

I end the phone call. I am in the carpark of Bunnings in my car. I am in a complete trance. I get out of the car and go inside. I don't even know what I am looking for here. All the items on the shelf look the same. I can make no sense of anything.

I walk out of there with nothing. I have completely forgotten why I came to Bunnings in the first place.

The lady asks to check my bag on the way out.

I open it for her, and she smiles at me.

'All good, thanks,' she says.

I look at her. This 20-something year old girl who is just starting her life. I look at her with envy. *My life has just finished, and yours is just starting*, I think as I walk back to my car.

I question Kevin when he gets home from work. We go through different scenarios as to what would be going on here. We conclude that Jules is confused. She is on antidepressants, and she is not thinking straight.

We start going through the history of Jules's life. Not once was there an instance where she dressed up as a girl or went for a swim and said she would prefer to wear a bikini. Not once did she play with a doll or experiment with my make-up or say she wished she didn't have a penis.

'Surely, we would have seen a sign somewhere?' I say to Kevin.

'Well, you would think so. I mean, Jules has never been that boy who wanted to play rugby or football or get into brawls. Some of the usual stereotypical male roles. Jules has always been sensitive and arty and loved doing things like calligraphy and Lego, but surely that doesn't make her a girl.'

That night, I took a sleeping tablet and go to bed in tears. I am hoping that tomorrow, Jules tells me this is just a joke. They are still going to be my perfect son. Nothing has changed.

PART THREE

THE DEVESTATION

TUESDAY 23 MARCH

I start crying from the moment I open my eyes. Everything still seems so surreal. This can't be true. It just can't! I am in total denial as to what is happening.

I manage to get out of bed. Just. I go downstairs and get Blue and strap him up ready for a walk.

I walk in a daze. I few people say 'Good morning' to me. I want to scream at them 'What is so fucking good about it?'

I just try to smile at them and continue my walk. I am doing everything on autopilot. I got my coffee and some bread and head back home.

Kevin is up now.

'How are you doing?' he says to me.

I don't want him to say that to me. I want him to say Jules has just phoned and this is all a big misunderstanding. Jules is not transgender. She just got confused about everything. Jules just likes to wear female clothes sometimes, that's all.

That would be fine then. I could deal with that. *Harry Styles wears women's clothing, and he is still a major hunk*, I think. *That can be like Jules.*

Kevin doesn't say this to me. He hasn't heard from Jules and neither have I.

'Don't bother coming into work today,' he says to me.

'No, I am going to come in,' I reply. 'I have to get my mind off this.'

I manage to get myself to work. I look like shit. I feel sick. A constant pain that is below my chest. I don't want to eat anything or do anything. I just want to shrivel up and die.

I can't seem to concentrate on anything. All I can think about is Jules.

Maybe it's just a phase and Jules will soon realise that he is really a boy and not a girl.

When I get home, I started scrolling the internet for anyone that might be in the same situation as me. There are hundreds and hundreds of sites. I can't believe there is so much information on this stuff.

It is mostly for people who want to transition, not so much for the parents of the person that is transitioning.

I discover a site called Parents of children with ROGD. Rapid Onset Gender Dysphoria.

So, this comes suddenly, I think. I read and read for hours. There are so many stories of parents who have lost their kids because of this—kids who refuse to have anything to do with their parents because the parents don't accept their decision. Most of these stories are of parents who are heartbroken, parents who are trying to accept their kids for who they want to be but don't fully believe it and certainly can't get used to it straight away. That sounds like me. But it's not fair for these parents. They had no idea, and now their children are practically disowning them because they did not support them.

I don't want to be like them, but I feel their pain.

How is it that I am part of this group now? This group of parents that had no idea that their kids were transgender? I never thought I would be part of this, and even while I am reading these articles, I still can't believe that I am one of those parents.

Will this be Jules and me? Will I lose Jules because I don't support her enough? Will I lose her because I don't accept this quick enough?

I can't lose my child because of this.

I looked at several other sites.

One is about transgenders and how they are all different in the way they transition. Some like to dress as their preferred gender in private and don't change their name or pronouns. Some like to transition socially but do not wish to take hormones or change their genitals. Some like to transition fully and take hormones to make them more feminine or male and also get bottom surgery.

No! Surely, Jules won't want to do all that. She won't take hormones and have bottom surgery and change their name and pronouns. She won't dress in skirts and dresses or wear make-up. That's not Jules! Jules is so reserved and hates any sort of attention. I mean, there is going to be major attention with this confession.

She will probably just dress the same and keep her body the same as it was and not much will change, except the fact that she is more feminine inside.

She will still be the same loving Jules. Quiet and reserved but much more fem than before.

I couldn't have been more wrong!

WEDNESDAY 24 MARCH

I prayed to God that I could die in my sleep last night. I still haven't heard from Jules. I guess she is giving me a lot of space. I woke up again in tears.

I walk the dog. He is oblivious to what's going on. *I wish I was Blue*, I think, as I walk him. I walk along the back streets of where I live. I don't want to run into anyone I know. Anyone who might ask me questions. Questions like 'How are the kids?', or even worse, 'how are you going?'

I can't face anyone who is happy. I no longer have any happiness in my life. I can't face anyone who doesn't have a transgender child. I can't face living.

I start cursing Jules silently. *You have done this to me! You have made me ill! You have made me want to die! You have ruined my life! How could you do this to me?*

I walk along the roads, and tears are streaming down my face. I am glad for the darkness of late March. The anonymity that it gives me. Nobody can see me. Nobody can see the endless stream of tears that won't stop. Nobody knows what is happening to me. Nobody can see my pain.

When I get home, Kevin is there. Usually, he would have gone to work by now, but he knows how bad I am. I know that he is so worried too, but I can only think of my own pain.

I go over all the 'This can't be happening. Maybe Jules is just confused' scenarios with Kevin, and he agrees with me. I guess we are both trying to reassure ourselves that Jules will change her mind.

I pull myself together and go to work. Nobody knows about Jules yet. Maybe they won't ever know? Maybe I never need to tell anybody?

The day is a complete blur of phone calls and invoicing and talking to customers. I look at the customers that come in, and I wonder if any of them have ever gone through what I am going through before. Have any of my customers had a child that came out of the blue and told them that he or she was transgender? How would they have coped with that? Would they just be like 'Yeah, I was all cool with that', or 'Well I am glad they are happy being their real self now'?

I am the only parent who thinks they could never get used to this and could never imagine their precious, brilliant boy transitioning into a girl.

Whenever I get a second, I get onto sites about transgenders. I want more information. I need to know what is going to happen here. I need to know that Jules won't change anything about herself. I convince myself that this is the case.

I started to learn all these terms that I never knew much about, because I never had to, or maybe just because I am ignorant. Things like non-binary and androgynous. I had seen models who would probably come under this umbrella but never thought much about it.

I mean, Jules could be like that. She has always had a very beautiful face. I used to think that Jules was not handsome but beautiful. I have seen lots of guys wearing make-up through my years. I mean, all the popstars of my era always wore make-up and dresses. Nobody would bat an eyelid, as it was just the way it was.

Maybe Jules just wants to put on a dress now and again and wear a bit of make-up. No big deal. Lots of males do that. I don't have a problem with Jules doing that sort of stuff I try to convince myself.

Jules just wants to dress more like a female at times. Even though I can't ever imagine this happening, it settles my stomach for now.

THURSDAY 25 MARCH

I pull myself out of bed. I start crying all over again. These thoughts are consuming me constantly. It's all I can think about all day and night. From the moment I wake up until I go to bed. It is in my head continuously. I can't think of anything else other than the fact that Jules is now transgender.

It is now Thursday. It's my day off work. I have survived three days of this so far. I don't even know how I have managed to. I am hoping that today will be the day when lightning strikes me down and it kills me instantly. Or maybe I cross the road and a truck knocks me over because it didn't see me. Maybe I just lie myself down on the train tracks and hope that it is quick. The only thing I would be concerned about there is that the train driver would never get over it.

Maybe by the weekend, Jules will tell me she has it all wrong and that she is not transgender.

I have an appointment with my hairdresser. I see her every four to five weeks. I never miss an appointment. I am very regimented like that.

I must look like shit because when I get there, she asks me if I am okay.

'Yes, I'm fine,' I lie. 'Just tired.'

'Is it River?'

'Yes,' I lie. I always have problems with River, so I can use her as my excuse today.

She is always getting into some sort of argument at school, whether it be with a teacher or student. There is always something.

The school isn't really equipped for autistic kids, even if they get funding, and trust me, this school is getting shitloads of funding for her. Still, I am always getting a phone call saying that River has spat at a teacher, or she threw her cupcake at another student, or better still, she just tried to cut her arm off with a pair of paper scissors. I don't even know if that would be possible, but nevertheless, I am always getting phone calls.

I get through the appointment without bursting into tears and get back into my car.

I feel sick, but I need to eat something. I grab a sandwich from a deli where I know I won't run into anyone I know and try and eat it in my car. Just when I am trying to stomach eating it, someone taps on my window. *Oh my god*, I think, *it's one of the people I used to work with several years ago.*

'Hey Jane,' he says. 'It's me, Brian, from the old housing loan centre? Remember me? We used to work together?'

'Oh yeah, Brian,' I manage to say to him unenthusiastically. 'Nice to see you.' I try to smile.

'Hey, how are you? How are the kids going?'

'Really well, thanks.' I lie to him. 'Yep, everyone is good.'

'You have two kids, right? A son and a daughter?'

If a tree could fall on my car now and kill me, it would be perfect timing.

'Yes, that's right. Jules and River,' I say, trying to smile. A son and a daughter, I think. No, that's not right. I have two daughters now. 'And yourself? Do you have kids?'

'Me, no. No kids. Never really wanted any,' he says.

I look at him as if to say, *Can you leave me alone now?*

'Well, good to see you' he says, 'You look really well.'

How is that even possible? I think. I look like complete shit!

'Good to see you too, Brian.' *I hope I never see you again in my life*, I think. *Then you would never ask me that question again.*

I try to eat the sandwich and get about halfway through before I start gagging. *I can't even get a sandwich down me*, I think. *Maybe starvation will kill me.*

I got home and ran inside and shut the door.

I start scrolling every site I can find on transgenders again. This is becoming a habit, but I need answers.

My hairdresser texts me. 'Are you okay Jane? You didn't look well today. I am always here if you need to talk to me, okay?'

She has no idea what is going on in my life. Never in her wildest dreams would she believe Jules is transgender. I mean, I don't.

'I am okay, thanks,' I say. 'It's just that life gets hard sometimes.'

'Well, anytime you need a chat,' she replies, 'I am here for you.'

I have been going to the same hairdresser for years, so no wonder she noticed I looked ill.

I have become obsessed with looking at sites with stories of parents who have just found out that their child is transgender.

A lot of these parents are like me. They had absolutely no idea that their child was transgender, and now their kids are rejecting them because they are unsupportive. Parents like me, I think. I am not supportive. I should say 'congratulations' to Jules and be happy that they are their true self.

No. I am one of those sad parents who will never get used to it.

Will I ever be able to get used to this? Will I ever be able to say that Jules is my daughter?

Maybe Jules will tell me soon that she is not transgender and this has all just been a huge mistake. Yes, that's what she will do. Then I can continue my life.

She can go back to being a boy and we can put all this behind us.

FRIDAY 26 MARCH

Kevin is off on his annual boy's trip.

There are about 30 guys who go every year for a few days. They say it's a golf trip, but I don't think anyone has ever played golf on the holiday. They just drink a lot and party for a few days. Kevin will then come back home exhausted and will have to go back to work and have a hangover for a week.

Well, he's been doing this for years, and he really enjoys it. It's his annual getaway with the boys.

I don't want him to go, as I need him here with me. I need him to tell me that Jules is not transgender and not to worry about it. I need him to tell me not to cry anymore because soon our boy will be back. He will be Julian again.

'Are you sure you don't want me to stay home?' he asks. I know he is worried about me, and I can see this is really affecting him too. He just wants to stay strong for all of us. He can see that I am beginning to fall apart but there is nothing I can do to stop it.

'Don't worry, I will be fine,' I try to reassure him.

'Okay, but I am only half an hour away if you need me,' he says reassuringly.

I meet Rochelle for breakfast. It is something we have done for many years. We meet for breakfast every Friday morning for a chat.

No different to any other Friday, except this time, Jules is a girl.

As soon as she sees me, she gives me a hug, and I start sobbing.

We sit at breakfast, and I can hardly eat a piece of toast let alone a full breakfast.

She listens to me while I talk and cry. She reassures me that Jules is only like this because of that bitch Sally.

'I mean, it's only since Jules met Sally that all his depression started. Then losing all that weight, and now being transgender? It's too much of a coincidence,' she says. 'Sally is the common denominator in all this. It's all her fault.'

She's right, I think. I mean, Rochelle is Jules's Godmother. She was there at the birth. She would have picked up something wrong there. Something that pointed to Jules being a girl. Perhaps not when Jules was born but later down the track. I mean, her son Blake went on so many holidays with us, and he was completely shocked when Rochelle said that Jules is transgender. That's just it. Not one person could have ever picked that. Certainly not me!

We sat there at breakfast for over an hour, me crying a lot and eating nothing and Rochelle listening.

She listens with sympathy, but she can't make this go away. Nobody can.

I wipe my tears and go to work. I am barely functioning, but work takes my mind away from thinking about Jules. It's the only thing that does at the moment.

Jules comes in around lunch time to my workplace.

She looks the same. Same clothes. Same long hair. Same Jules.

'Have you accepted it yet?' she asks me.

'No, Jules, I haven't got my head around it. I need a lot more time than a few days. But I was thinking, maybe you're not transgender? Maybe you are just non-binary or something like that?'

I know what I am doing. I am bartering with her.

'Maybe you just don't realise, honey, but you are really a boy that's non-binary. Just maybe a bit gender-fluid.'

'I am transgender, Mum, and you need to just accept that.'

'I can't.' I plead with her to stop this nonsense. 'Please Jules. Maybe you just think you are?'

She leaves my office to go and heads towards her car.

I put on my sunglasses on to hide my tears and ran after her.

I am on the street with her, begging her to change her mind. If not for her, then at least for me because I can't live like this.

'I can't live like this either!' she screams at me. 'I have had to live like this for 21 years, and I don't want to live like this any longer.'

'You have only just started to feel this way. It might be a mistake. I mean, how do you know for sure?'

'Because I have always known.'

'Well, why haven't I ever seen any sign of it?' I cry. 'You have never mentioned it to me. How the fuck could I not know?'

My friend Sandy drives past us and beeps her car horn and waves.

She has no idea what's going on. No idea that I am crying and begging Jules to change her mind about being transgender.

'Just accept it, Mum. It's not going to change.'

She gets in her car and drives away.

I go inside and wait 10 minutes before ringing her. I feel so bad for her feeling like this, but I can't help feeling the way I feel. I just want her to understand. I want her to give me time to accept this. I can't accept this yet. Not right now. Why the urgency? I don't understand.

She answers the third time I ring.

'I just want to make sure you are okay.' The tears are streaming down my face hard and fast.

'No, I am not okay, Mum. I just want you to realise that this is who I am. I am a girl, and that is not going to change!'

'But maybe you just think you are. Maybe you just like to wear girl's clothes?' I splutter.

'I like to wear girl's clothes because I am a girl!' she screams down the phone at me. 'I will talk about it with you when you get home from work.' Jules finishes the conversation.

I pull myself together somehow and go back into the office.

It's Friday, and we always order some takeout at work on Fridays. Today, we are having burgers.

'Lunch is ready,' one of the guys calls to me. My mind is elsewhere. I am in another world where this is not happening to me.

I go into the lunchroom. They are all eating and looking very happy because it's Friday. I mean, everyone loves Fridays, right?

I look at my burger. I feel like I am going to gag.

I can't eat a bite of eat. I feel ill.

'What's up?' Jason ask. He is one of our employees. 'Not hungry?'

'Just feeling a bit sick.' That's the understatement of the year!

'Maybe you just miss Kevin,' he jokes.

I don't laugh. I can't! I might never laugh again in my whole life.

I try to smile at him. I hope he can't see that I have been crying.

When I finish work, I race home and shut the door. I'm safe. I don't have to face anybody. I can shut the world out. If I never have to see anybody, then I never have to explain this to them.

Jules is waiting for me. I keep hoping with every ounce of my being that she is going to tell me this is not happening.

'Are you okay?' she asks me when I sit down.

'Not really,' I don't lie to her.

'Look,' she says, 'we can get through this, Mum, but I am not going to change my mind. I know who I am supposed to be and that I am a girl inside. I have known this for a very, very long time.'

'Well, what sort of mother am I if I have never picked up on this? Not even the slightest?' I am crying again.

'It's not your fault, Mum. I never really wanted you to pick up on it. I didn't even know why I was having these thoughts. I couldn't understand why I was having these thoughts. They were just always there.'

'Even when you were at a boy's school? I mean, what about when you were in the boys toilets? What did you do then?'

'I always used a cubicle.'

I know Jules has always been private, but I never really thought about Jules, as a boy, not liking his penis. So much that Jules had to hide away from the other boys. I didn't know she was a girl. How could I?

'I studied so much at school to stop any thoughts of this being in my mind,' she continued. 'I thought these ideas of wearing girls' clothes and being a girl might go away, but they never did.'

I feel sad. Exhausted and sad. *At least we are talking*, I think. *I don't want to lose Jules.*

I never want to lose Jules.

Jules says she is going to stay at Sally's house for the night. It is probably the best thing.

I sit on the couch, and I drink. A lot. I usually have a glass or two of wine every night, but I have started drinking a lot more.

I have even taken to having a quick shot or two of liquor in the morning.

There might be a big drinking problem happening there, but I couldn't give a shit. Maybe I will die of alcohol poisoning. That would be an easy escape. Then I would never have to think about this again.

River asks me if I'm okay.

I haven't told her about what is going on yet because I don't truly believe it myself. She can clearly see that I am not well.

'Yes, I am fine honey. All good,' I lied.

I started watching *Wayne's World* on Netflix. That show always made me laugh. Not tonight, I think.

I sit there crying.

I texted Tess. It's around 10 pm

'Are you awake?'

The reply comes quickly, which is unusual for Tess. She is pretty slow to reply to texts usually, but she probably knows there is something up.

'What is it?'

She knows I never stay awake this long at night. I am usually a nine o'clock at the latest type of girl.

'It's Jules,' I reply.

'What about him?'

'Jules is transgender.'

'Oh, thank goodness he's not sick,' comes the reply. 'I thought you were going to say Jules has cancer or something.'

We arranged to meet the next day for a walk. I tell her I don't want to stop anywhere for breakfast or coffee. I just want to walk. I can't bear the thought of running into anyone I know. Anyone who has their son with them. Their son who is always going to be their son and not suddenly change into their daughter.

SATURDAY 27 MARCH

I met up with Tess in the park near our houses. We only live a street apart, so it's easier for us both to meet in the middle.

When she sees me, she runs towards me and gives me a hug. I start crying, still not fully comprehending what is happening in my life.

I cry, and she listens. She tells me that after our texts last night, she realised the enormity of my confession and she sobbed her heart out. Tess is quite an emotional girl, so it would have hit her hard.

'Why did Jules never mention this to you?'

'I just don't know,' I sob. 'Maybe Jules thought things would change and that she might not feel this way forever?'

'But not even a hint of it?' she questions. 'I mean, I am angry with Jules for just springing this on you without any warning whatsoever. You walked with Jules every morning of their life, for God's sake, and not once did she mention any of this?'

'No.'

'It's insane. I mean, we were all totally in the dark about this one. I thought maybe Jules was gay but not transgender!'

'I know. I thought maybe she was gay too, but I never expected this! I mean, she could have given me at least some indication. Maybe something like "Mum, I feel like I want to wear women's clothes" or maybe "Mum, I feel very feminine at times." Something! Anything that might have prepared me for this massive curve ball. I mean, I don't even know where to begin with this.'

'I don't know,' Tess says. 'Do you think I should contact Jules and tell her that I am okay with all this? I mean, I don't want Jules to think that we are not supportive on this, right?'

Jules tutors my niece for maths, so Tess doesn't want her to feel uncomfortable when she comes to the house.

'That would be really nice,' I say 'Thanks. I am sure Jules would really appreciate that.'

We say our goodbyes, and Tess tells me to contact her if I need anything.

I tell her thanks before I head inside the house. I know what I need. Someone to tell me this is not true. Someone to tell me this is just a silly joke!

I feel devastated.
I feel exhausted.
I feel sad.
Like someone has died.
Like losing a son.

I have a drink and start to scroll the transgender sites again. This has become a very unhealthy addiction. So many stories. I can't believe this has happened to so many people. How was I so ignorant of what was happening around me? I guess I never had to think about it before.

I read that some parents grieve for the loss of their child. Like losing a son but gaining a daughter, or the other way around.

Some parents feel so sad that they want to commit suicide from the confession. Others say that after the initial grieving stage, they get used to it. They become closer to the child than before, because the child is now the gender they want to be, and they are much happier in themselves. They are much happier being the gender that they were born into.

I can't feel like that! Who are these parents? How does it then become the new normal for them to have a child who has changed their gender on them? How will I ever feel like that? How will I ever be close to Jules again?

How can I be close to Jules as my daughter and not my son? None of it makes any sense.

I have lost my son. I will never be happy again.

Sandy rings me

I pick up.

'What you up to? You want to catch up for a drink later?'

Silence

'What's the matter? Are you okay Jane? What's wrong?'

'Jules is transgender.'

'Oh my god,' she says. 'I had no idea. Did you know? Are you okay with that?'

'No,' I cry 'I didn't have any idea, and I am not okay with it.'

'Are you worried about what people will say?'

'Yes,' I cry. 'Yes I am.'

'I'm coming over.'

Sandy comes over an hour later with a heap of pre-made gin and tonics.

We sit on my couch while I cry and we both drink.

'I can't believe this,' I say to her 'I had no idea. I mean, there wasn't even a hint that Jules was transgender.'

I drink and cry, and she sits there silently listening to me.

A little later in the afternoon, Jules comes home.

I want to hug her, but I can't bring myself to do it. I am sure she doesn't want to hug me, anyway.

'I am going to tell my friends,' she announces to me.

Oh no, I think. This can't be happening so soon. So now everyone is going to know. Everyone will know Jules is transgender. This can't be Jules. Well, not the one I know anyway. Jules is such a private person. Surely, she wouldn't want all her friends to know this already.

'What, today?' I say to her.

'Yes. They are coming over soon.'

Sandy gives Jules a hug and says she is happy for her.

It's a beautiful gesture on her behalf, but I can't bring myself to say or do anything that even comes close to a celebratory hug or compliment. I wish I could, but I can barely breathe.

A few of Jules's friends come over. She has told them the news already, and they are all happy for her. They are congratulating her. Some are quite teary and are hugging her. *She looks exactly the same as before*, I think. This can't be real. This can't be my life now!

'Jules is not a girl!' I want to scream at these people.

I remain silent. Defeated. Sad.

Later, Sandy goes home and so do Jules's friends.

It's just the two of us now.

Jules's tells me that she has been calling herself Julie for some time now. She has been using this name at university and at Sally's house. She has also been using it around Sally's friends, and they have all accepted that she is Julie and not Julian.

So all of Sally's friends and her parents know that Jules is actually Julie.

That's just fucking brilliant! Everyone knows that Julian is Julie except for me.

That's not the name that I would have named her if she was born a girl at birth. She knew that I had Indiana picked out if she was a girl, not Julie.

74

This is unbelievable. How could all this be happening when I had no idea at all? How could all these other people be calling her Julie when I didn't know? How could that bitch and her family take this on board like it's nothing!

Jules tells me that Sally's family are very accepting of her being transgender and they always call her by her preferred name.

'Well, of course, they are accepting,' I yell at her. 'That's because it's not their fucking child, is it?'

Jules tells me once again that things are not going to change, and I really need to start getting used to this.

She leaves to go back to Sally's house, and once again, I sit on the floor of my kitchen and sob and sob until there are no more tears left.

SUNDAY 28 MARCH

I wait all day for Kevin to come home from his boy's trip.

I try to watch a football match for the team that I back, but I can't focus on anything. The tears keep streaming down my face.

Tess keeps texting me and asking me if I am okay.

I lie and tell her I am fine. She knows I'm not, but she also knows I don't want to see anyone either.

Kevin comes home around 4 pm.

He is exhausted from his boy's trip, but I can tell he is not in the right frame of mind. There is sadness in his eyes. He has probably drunk way too much beer and is feeling tired, but I can tell he is worried. Very worried.

Jules comes home a little later with Sally in tow. They have come to grab some of Jules's stuff. I am at the point where I can hardly speak to either of them now. I don't even say hello.

It doesn't make any difference anyway, because Jules is constantly angry with me. Constantly wanting me to accept this quickly so we can both get on with our lives.

Jules comes downstairs while I sit on the couch crying. She is wearing the same baggy clothes as always and looks no different at all.

I ask her if she is going to change the way she dresses at all, and she tells me probably not.

I don't know whether she is just saying this to keep the peace with all of us or whether she is saying this for real.

'Well, if you are not going to change anything about yourself, then I don't need to tell everyone right?' I say to her. I have been reading a lot of articles on the way some parents barter with their kids when they tell them they are transgender.

They try to ask their kids only to wear certain clothes around the house and not out in public. They say that they will use their chosen name at home but not out in public. I realise this is exactly what I am doing now. I am bartering with Jules.

She is extremely angry now. 'I don't know what I will change, but whatever it is, you need to get used to it,' she screams at me.

She grabs her stuff, and they both hurry out of the door and head to the car.

I sit there crying as I hear them go.

I have never had so many arguments with Jules in my life.

After they leave, I turn to Kevin, who is sitting on the couch next to me.

'What happens if she wants to go on hormones?'

'That's not going to happen. Jules is on antidepressant medication. No doctor will put them on hormones straight away,' He says. 'Don't worry about that now. That is way down the track, and that's if it happens at all.'

'Yeah, I guess you're right,' I say. 'She won't be able to do that yet'.

I am satisfied with this answer. Kevin is right. She can't start changing her body if she is not of sound mind.

Antidepressants alter your mood, so she would have to go off them first. That will take some time, so at least then she has time to think about this before rushing into it.

I take a sleeping tablet and go to bed and cry. With the extra alcohol and sleeping tablet, I am knocked out.

I wake to yelling and a loud screeching noise outside my window. A car has stopped at the end of our street. We live in a quiet street that has a dead end, so nobody can get through from there. You would have to turn the car around.

Another car comes to a halt, and a man gets outside and starts yelling, 'Get the fuck out of the car.'

He repeats this over and over to the girl in the other parked car.

I peek out of my window.

She stopped the car and has locked the door.

Some of the neighbours have come out of their houses outside onto the street. Kevin goes outside too.

The man is desperate.

'Please help me,' he pleads. 'My daughter is on drugs, and I have a tracker on her car. She has got mixed up with the wrong crowd, and now she is on meth.' He is so shaken he is crying. 'She has just finished year 12, and she is at university, and now she is on drugs! She was a straight A student!'

I listen, and I feel the man's pain as I lie there. He would have no idea as to what is going on in our lives. He can't control his child anymore, and I can't control mine.

I feel nothing but sadness for him. I feel hatred towards his daughter! How selfish!

These parents give their kids everything these days. A private education, money, cars, a good home to live in, and this is how they repay us.

The girl eventually gets out of the car when her uncle arrives. Her father grabs her and puts her in the passenger seat of his car.

He just wants his daughter back. I just want my son.

I cry myself back to sleep. I cry for my miserable life. I cry for his miserable life. *There is no hope*, I think. *God, please take me in my sleep. Please don't let me wake up.*

MONDAY 29 MARCH

I wake up and take Blue for a walk. Alone and in the dark. Down the back streets where I won't run into anyone.

Thank goodness it is getting a bit darker in the mornings. Soon enough, winter will arrive, and I will run into no one in the mornings. It will be too cold and too dark.

When I get back home, I ask Kevin, 'Should we tell our employees at work? I mean, they can see that we are not doing well. Maybe they are wondering what's going on?'

We are a very small business with only a handful of employees. I am sure they would have noticed that not all is well in our world.

He agrees, and I send the message out to all of them.

Hi guys. Just letting you know that Jules has come out transgender, and we are supporting her as best we can. (I wish I could believe that part, I think)

Please be supportive of Jules and of Kevin and me as it is a very tough thing to deal with as a family.

Please don't mention this to me at work as I am very upset now and find it very hard to talk to anyone about this.

I hope you appreciate that we need time to work through this, and I am thanking you in advance for your support.

They all come back with texts like, 'It's all good, Jane' and 'We are here for you' and 'we support you.'

The replies make me cry even more.

We tell River. She is like, 'Oh, okay, so she's my sister now.'

She doesn't even blink as she heads off to school, not thinking twice about what being transgender entails. I am sure there are many of them at the school where she goes. It doesn't bother her at all.

Kevin says maybe we should send out a message to the family now too. I think he is right, as I don't want them to think that there is something wrong if they see me and I am a total train wreck!

I sent a similar message out to the family members. All of them except my mum and dad and Kevin's mother. His father passed away 13 years ago, so it's just his mum now.

They all come back with supportive messages of 'We are here for you' and 'Let me know if you want to talk about it.'

I put on my message not to ring me as I am so upset. I can't talk. They oblige my wishes and only respond to me by texts.

I get through the day at work, somehow.

The guys all gave me a hug, and I tried my best not to cry.

I focus on my work so I can stop thinking about Jules. Every thought is consumed by her. I cannot think of anything else.

I look at the guys at work and think, *Why don't they think like that? Why aren't they transgender? Why is this happening to my son and not to someone else's? Why me? Life is so unfair!*

I manage to get through the day, and as soon as I get home, I shut the door and go inside and get a drink. Once again, I start scrolling transgender sites. I read some stories where the transgender person has detransitioned. Is that good or bad? I guess it would be fine if you hadn't gone the full way and had hormones and surgery, but what happens if you had? How can you detransition from that?

The more I read, the more confusing it becomes. Some transgenders do the hormones but not surgery. Some do both. Some do none of these things. What will Jules do? Will she choose hormones and surgery or none of it?

I am exhausted from going from site to site reading people's stories. They are all sad, whether they transition or not.

WEEK 2

Jules came home on Thursday and brought Sally with her. It's my day off work, so I am at home, hiding from the outside world. I really haven't seen much of either of them, as I guess they are both staying away from me because I am in denial, and on top of that, I am a blubbering mess! Constantly.

I am in the laundry doing the washing. I am crying again as usual.

Jules comes down and asks me if I'm okay.

'I just want my son back,' I cry.

'I am not your son! You can't call me your son anymore.'

I cry so much I just about collapse.

Jules holds onto me and tries to calm me down.

I am crying on her shoulder, not standing up straight as I'm unable to.

'You need to call me your daughter now,' Jules says to me, as she keeps me standing upright.

'My daughter? You have always been my perfect son.'

'I am not your son anymore, Mum. You need to get used to calling me your daughter.'

I just nod. 'Can I still call you Jules?'

'Yes, you can always call me that,' Jules says reassuringly.

We hugged for a while, and then Jules pulled away telling me it would be okay.

I wish I could believe her.

She goes back upstairs and shuts her bedroom door. I am sure she is reporting back to Sally about how our conversation went.

Later, Jules comes downstairs to talk to me about what is going on for Sally's birthday.

I had completely forgotten, as I haven't thought about anything else other than Jules being transgender.

'Are we still going out tomorrow night for Sally's birthday?' she asks.

We had planned this a few weeks ago. This was before the confession.

I thought they both might not want to go, but I was wrong. I certainly didn't feel like going out to dinner. I didn't feel like leaving the house. In fact, I didn't feel like living anymore, but I say okay.

The next day, Jules rings me at work. She wants to wear a dress to dinner.

I nearly fall off my chair. I have never seen Jules wear anything other than baggy shorts and cargo pants and polo shirts.

I don't know if I can deal with this, especially not at the moment.

I tell Kevin. He looks at me like, *What the fuck.*

'No,' he says, 'I am not comfortable with that.'

I tell Jules later that neither of us are ready for that yet.

The four of us go out to dinner. River doesn't like social events much, so she stays at home.

In hindsight, this is a good thing, because it is uncomfortable from the minute we get in the car.

The fact that Jules could not wear a dress pisses her off already.

I mean, we are doing this for her. We don't really like Sally all that much, to say the least. She has no conversation skills whatsoever, and her lack of personality doesn't help either.

The dinner was a catastrophe to say the least.

Jules wouldn't speak to us to start with, and now she is staring angrily at us, as we both do our best to make conversation.

We are making some jokes about when we used to go camping and talking about our holidays as a family. We are talking about Jules in Legoland and how it was the best trip ever. We are just trying to keep the conversation flowing, as neither of them are making any effort.

We are focusing on Jules, but we are using the wrong pronouns. We didn't realise that pronouns should change when you are talking about their past. We were talking as if Jules was a boy in their childhood.

Are we being ignorant?

But Jules's photos are all of us being together on the beach and playing in the sand and having fun. In all these pictures, Jules is in boardshorts and no top. Jules is in stereotypically boy's clothes. There are no pictures of Jules in her pretty pink dress and matching shoes or Jules in her bikini.

We did not realise that we had to change the past tense as well to suit how she feels now? I mean, how are we supposed to know that?

We get home from the worst night out ever, and Jules and Sally go upstairs.

I sit on the couch with Kevin. I think the two of us are in shock.

I mean, we only just found out that Jules is a girl, and now we must change her past pronouns to suit the present. Both of us are totally confused.

'Well, that went well,' Kevin says as he grabs a beer.

'What a fucking nightmare.' I turn to him with an exasperated look on my face.

'Well, it's not us that wanted to go,' he says. 'I mean, we were only doing this because Jules said it would be a nice thing to do for Sally, right?'

'Yeah,' I agree. 'I certainly didn't want to go out with them. It was their idea, and now we are these terrible parents that can't use the right pronouns!'

Jules comes downstairs. She is very, very angry. That makes two of us!

She sits on the chair next to us with a defiant look on her face and her arms crossed.

She starts out by telling us we are using the wrong pronouns.

'Well, okay, mate,' Kevin says. 'I'm sorry, but we didn't realise. We are trying to understand.'

'If you don't want to be part of this journey with me, then tell me now.'

'We do want to be part of this journey with you, Jules. It's just hard for me and your mum to know exactly what we are supposed to do here.'

'I don't want to be referred to as a boy, anymore. I want to forget all my past. I don't want to remember anything before I came out as a girl.'

I sit on the couch stoned faced.

What a complete bitch!

I start to rant at her. 'Well, I will just erase all your past then! All those awards you won that were in the name of Julian that are on the cabinets, I will throw them all away. All the photos from your past. All the holidays we went on together as a family. The diaries we made together with pictures and shells and drawings. I will just throw them all in the fucking bin! Then you won't have to remember any of your fucking past!' I scream. 'You can erase the whole fucking thing!'

'No that's not what I mean!'

'Well, what do you fucking mean, then?'

Kevin starts to interrupt. 'Let's not argue about this,' he says calmly. 'We will support you in your journey, Jules. We just need a bit of time.'

She looks at me. I sit there in silence, not knowing if I can be part of this journey. I stare at the TV and say nothing.

She continues to stare at me, but I am not giving in. All I ever did was take her everywhere she wanted to go and do everything she wanted to do. She wanted to go to

Legoland, then I would make it happen. If she wanted to go to Disneyland, I would make it happen. In fact, I would do everything in my power to make her happy, regardless of how much it cost or how much time it took. I can't count how many times I trudged after her to a Lego store and filled up buckets and buckets of pieces that she needed. How I would go to places that she wanted to go even though it took us hours to get there. Nothing was too much trouble. Her whole childhood has been me trying to make her happy, and now she is throwing everything back in my face. Just because she is a girl doesn't mean she should erase her past. And how the fuck were we meant to know that we had to change the pronouns even in past tense?

Is there an instruction book on this? If so, I am sure it would read something like this, 'When your child comes out as transgender then you must immediately refer to any of their past tense with the correct pronouns.'

Jules gets up and goes back upstairs.

I look over at Kevin.

He is at a loss for words. This must be so hard on him. His son telling him that she is now his daughter. I can't feel his pain, though. I am in too much pain myself.

Could this get any worse? I think, as I go to bed.

Once again, I cry and pray to die in my sleep. I pray to God that I don't wake up.

I am not strong enough to deal with this, I plead to God. I can't do this! If there is a God, then I pray for him to let me die in my sleep. I pray for him to let me never wake up.

WEEK 3

I struggle through the week still being in denial of everything that is happening to me.

I have now texted my other friend Janine (who also suspected Jules might be gay) about what is going on. I told her not to ring me, as I am way too upset to talk.

Now, all my friends and most of my family know. They know I don't want to be contacted, and they all just text me to see if I'm okay. I'm not but I tell them that I am.

Tuesday comes, and I am in the kitchen trying to cook without crying.

Jules and Sally are also in the kitchen, giggling and carrying on while they are cooking.

I can't stand to be near Sally anymore, and I hate her being in my house, but on the other hand, I want her to be there for Jules, as I just can't deal with her by myself.

They are both looking at Jules's phone. I ask them what they are looking at.

Jules tells me she is changing her name on her Facebook profile.

I ask her why she needs to do that.

She tells me that she might as well start now by changing her name on her social media accounts.

I say to her that she doesn't even like social media, so why bother with it now?

This is true, as Jules has always said that she hates social media because people always look so false on there and pretend that they are happy when they are not.

She says she's doing it anyway.

I am freaking out now, as I think that a lot of my acquaintances are also linked with her account. Not only that, but I have tagged Jules in a lot of my holiday posts.

I check my Facebook account. Every single one of my posts with Jules tagged in have now changed to Julie Foster.

The profile picture of Jules has changed also. It's Jules in a dark blue dress. I have never seen Jules dressed up like this before.

I am panicking. I haven't even had time to think about this side of things.

I change the settings on my account to private, then I realise that people that I am friends with can still see all my posts.

I started deleting people off my account. People that I really don't see at all. Just people from my past. Surely, they won't notice.

I can't believe how fast this is all happening.

Later that night I wrote Jules a letter. It reads:

Dear Jules

I had a discussion last night with your dad about you changing your name on Facebook. I find this quite strange that you feel a need to do this, as you have always been a person that despised social media.

I hope you realise by doing this, people will find out, and it will be in the most shocking way possible.

All your cousins that are still in America, my beautician, hairdresser, your Auntie and possibly your grandma and grandad.

Also, I have tagged you in a lot of my posts which now read 'Julie.'

I know you feel that you need to let the world know that you are a girl now but your dad and I are not able to deal with this yet.

I have thought about closing my Facebook down, but it is linked to the business, which I use for advertising.

I don't feel like I can discuss this with certain people on my Facebook when they have found out this way. I am not ready for that yet.

Can you please rethink this and maybe set up a new profile or change the name back for now?

We are trying to support you as much as we can, but please be mindful of us in this stressful situation and how something like this can impact so many lives in so many ways.

Love Mum. xx

I put this note by Jules's bedroom door so she can read it when she wakes up.

I go to bed feeling very, very sick and very, very upset.

I go to work the next day. Jules comes in and says that she will start up a separate profile, a new one that is not linked to me at all. I ask her to not send me a friend request me, as I can't deal with it now. She says that she won't. I also ask her not to send one to any of my friends either. She says she won't.

I am happy that she is prepared to do this for me but wonder how long it will be before everyone knows. I still cannot even talk about this without crying, and I have no idea when or if I will ever be able to deal with it.

Friday comes, and I am grabbing a coffee before work. I run into Sandy. She tells me she has had a friend request from Julie Foster. I don't understand at first, but she then says its Jules. I am shocked beyond belief. I start to cry and ask her not to accept it. How many other friends of mine has she sent friend requests?

I call her, and when she answers, I start questioning her as to why she is sending friend requests to all my friends.

She says she doesn't really understand social media sites that well and got one of her friends at university to help her with it.

'Stop sending friend requests to all my friends!' I yell down the phone 'You said you wouldn't do this.'

I am so upset that I can't talk to her anymore and hang up.

When I get home, she does apologise to me about it and tells me she has deleted all those requests.

I take a breath of relief, but the worst is yet to come.

It's Saturday

I haven't been anywhere for days, except to work and back and outside to walk the dog. If I need groceries, I go to a shop that's a bit out of town where I know I will not run into anybody. I still can't face anyone yet and can't stop crying. Every time I see a mother or a father out with their son, I cry. I am envious that their son is still their son while I am quietly grieving for mine.

Even when I walk Blue, I see families walking together. They all seem to be laughing and enjoying each other's company.

They couldn't even comprehend what my life is like. How, in the blink of an eye, everything can change totally. Your past is not the same. Your present is uncertain, and the future is something I can't even bring myself to think about.

This is what I used to be like before I think. Before all this happened. Before Jules met Sally. Before, when Jules was a boy. Before Jules came out as transgender.

It's Tuesday night, and Jules and Sally are at home upstairs in Jules's bedroom.

Jules comes downstairs and announces that she is going to start hormone treatment.

I am in shock. How can this happen so soon? Don't that have to live socially like the opposite sex for a certain period of time? I mean, it hasn't even been a month.

'But you have only been transgender for a month,' comes my reply.

'I have been transgender all my life.'

'Well, surely they can't put you on them straight away?'

'Yes, they can'

'But you are still on antidepressants?'

'I know what I'm doing, Mum. It doesn't make any dif-ference that I'm on antidepressants. I know what I want!' Jules is raising her voice now. 'I am a girl, and I want the body of a girl!'

'It's too soon' I am crying again. 'You might change your mind. It might be a mistake'.

'It's not a mistake, Mum. I have thought about this for a very long time, and I know it's what I want to do.'

'What happens if it's not the right decision? Is it reversible?'

'It is the right decision, and it's not reversible,' she says.

I did not expect this. Not this soon, maybe not ever.

I start reading everything on hormones for transgen-ders, and I am blown away by what they can do. I mean,

Jules can get breasts and softer skin and even curves from these hormones.

I am not ready for this. I might never be ready for this. How am I ever going to get used to this?

I tell Kevin when he gets home. He is as shocked as I am.

'Really, this soon?' he says, 'I didn't think they would do that if Jules is still on the antidepressants?'

'Neither did I, but Jules is going on them and very soon.'

'Well, what happens if it's not the right decision?' Kevin asks. He sounds very concerned and overwhelmed that this can happen so quickly.

'I don't know. I hope it is the right decision. I guess there is nothing we can do. Jules is an adult.'

Kevin agrees, but we both sit there completely stunned by the realisation that pretty soon, Jules will have breasts.

I go to bed with my mind whirling. This is all going way too fast. I can't even comprehend that Jules is transgender and now she is going on hormones. This can't be real, I think.

I dreamt that night. I dreamt that Jules is my boy again. That he comes bounding down the stairs with a huge smile on his face. Fit and healthy and ready to go and play badminton with his mates. He smiles at me and tells me to keep his dinner in the fridge as he will eat it when he gets home.

The next morning, I awaken to the same nightmare.

It's Sunday, and Jules has come back home to talk to me. She comes into my room and says she has something she needs to talk to me about.

I wait in anticipation for the next blow, trying not to get teary.

'What is it?'

'Do you want grandchildren?'

'Not really. Why are you asking me that?' I hadn't thought much about having grandchildren. It was never my grand plan in life. I didn't even think about the hormones affecting Jules's sperm count but of course it would.

'I don't want them, but I thought I would ask you first before I go onto hormones,' she tells me.

I have never even thought about having grandkids, but I never thought I would be questioned about it in this way. I always thought that I would just get old and just enjoy my life. I don't really want little children in my life as I pictured myself doing other things.

I picture going to South Africa and checking out all the wildlife. Going to the Amazon and Antarctica. Getting on a boat and travelling around the world exploring of all the little uninhabited islands along the way. I mean, we have always done a lot of travelling with the children when they were younger and even in their teens, but these are going to be long trips away from home. Still, this is my life I'm talking about and not Jules's.

'Don't you want any, though?' I question her. 'I mean, you are only 21. I didn't want any kids when I was your age, but later in life, I did. You can't make a decision like that at this age. You have no idea how you are going to feel when you get older.'

'I know I don't want kids,' she says defiantly 'I have never wanted them, and I never will.'

'It's only because she doesn't want them. Because she doesn't have a fanny, I think.'

'It's nothing to do with Sally not wanting them. I have never wanted them either. I can save my sperm if I have any, but I really don't want to do that.'

'It's your body. You do what you want with it.' I finish the conversation.

After she leaves, I start going completely crazy!

It's not the fact that she doesn't want children. It's the fact that she is not changing her mind on being transgender.

I search her bedroom. I turn everything upside down. I am looking for any clues. Anything that can confirm or even raise the slightest doubt that she is a girl and always has been.

I need evidence. Even the slightest bit of evidence that points to the fact that she is transgender.

The only thing I can find is a stereotypical girls' Lego set. That's it! That's all I can find.

I ring Rochelle and tell her what has just happened. She is shocked and doesn't know what to say to me. She listens to me blubber and cry on the other end of the phone. She has no words to console me. She is as shocked as I am. She says she would have never picked this to happen. Neither did I. These things happen to other people. Not to me. Not to Jules. Not to our family.

Jules came back that day to pick up some other stuff so she could go and stay at Sally's for a few days. Away from me, I guess. I can't blame her. I am a complete mess!

I confronted her outside her room.

'What exactly are you looking for?' she asks me.

'Anything to confirm that you are a girl, and there is nothing in your room to confirm that.'

'What difference does it make if you find anything or not? It doesn't prove anything.'

'Yes, it does,' I scream.

'I was very good at hiding things.'

'Like what? Did you used to get dressed up in my clothes when I wasn't home?' I question her. 'Or maybe use my make-up? Or pretend to be a girl?'

'I am a girl, and yes, I used to do those things.' She is shouting at me now.

'Well, why didn't I ever know? Why did I never see any-thing like that happening?'

'Because I'm smart. I was very good at covering up everything I did.'

'Even when you were little?' I scream.

'Yes,' Jules says calmly.

'Why didn't you just tell me?'

'Because I heard you and Dad talking one day when you were watching TV. You saw a kid come on the TV who was transgender, and you said to Dad that it would be so hard for the parents to deal with that situation.'

'That's it? That's the only reason you didn't tell me? That's the only fucking reason you thought not to mention this to me?'

'Yes.'

'Well, it is fucking hard on the parents,' I am crying now. 'Especially when they had no fucking idea!'

'Well, it's fucking hard for me too,' she screams. 'I am the one who has to live with this curse!'

She turns to leave. 'I am going, and I won't be coming back.'

'Is this why you asked me about your bank accounts?'

'Yes.'

'So you thought I would take all your money from you? You really think I am that parent? That parent who takes whatever money you have in your bank accounts and then throws you out of the house? You think I am that parent who would turn my back on you because of this?'

'Maybe.'

'How could you possibly think that of me? I am not that parent. I am a parent that needs more time to get used to this, but I am not going to turn my back on you!' I yell. 'I am not going to lose a child over this. You could walk out of that door and not come back, or not talk to me for years, and I would still welcome you back with open arms. You have to give me time to get used to this.' I am pleading with Jules now. 'It's only been a couple of weeks, for God's sake. How can any parent get used to this that quickly?'

'Some parents do,' she says calmly.

'What fucking parents? Where are these fucking parents who can get used to this in a matter of weeks?'

'I'm going now,' she says. 'Otherwise, we will just continue to argue.'

After she leaves, I go to my bedroom. I lay on the bed in a heap, sobbing and heaving. I can't stop. This is all so surreal. I can't live like this. I can't cope with this. I will never get used to this. Blue jumps up on the bed as if to comfort me. God, I wish I was a dog.

I don't know if River has heard us arguing, but I am sure she realises what is going on. This is not something that ever happens in our household, and even if she doesn't hear it, I am sure she can feel the tension in the air.

I go through the working week in a complete daze. I have not heard from Jules, but it's probably for the best, as we just can't stop arguing with each other. It is a constant argument of when I am going to accept this and how soon I can do that.

I manage to get through each day, but I have no idea how I am doing it. I cry all the time. I still can't eat properly. I constantly feel sick. I am in a constant state of disbelief as to what is happening. It is almost like I am looking outside my body wondering who this person is. Only a month ago, I was just a normal parent doing normal parent things. Now, I am a total mess of a mother who can't get through a day without crying.

Jules doesn't come back home until Thursday.

It is the day before Easter Break.

We are going on the boat to our usual little island getaway.

I don't want to go, but Kevin says it will do me good.

I am about to go and get some groceries from the shop, the one where I never run into anyone, when I get a phone call from River's school.

This is not unusual, as she gets into a bit of trouble from time to time being autistic. The school says she is at the nurse's station and has threatened to kill herself.

I go to the school to pick her up. My head is in a complete daze. I just don't know how to cope with this now, on top of everything else.

I try to stay calm as I listen to the teacher telling me that River wants to throw herself off the top of the school building. I am trying not to cry.

He tells me the only reason she doesn't is because it will hurt her sister so much.

Her sister, I think. *This is just too much!*

He suggests that she needs to see a doctor or an emergency nurse as soon as possible, as this is very serious.

I go to emergency. I am sitting there in the waiting room, wondering if anyone else here is in the same situation as me. It's almost laughable. How would anyone else here ever be in this same situation?

I look around me at other people who are waiting. Some are holding different parts of their bodies with aches and pains. Some are bleeding. Some are finding it hard to breathe. Nobody is there because their child wants to throw themselves off a building. Nobody is there because their kid is transgender and they had no idea about it. Nobody is going through the same thing as I am.

People are there, because their injuries are physical. The injuries for the people in my life are not physical. They can never be seen, but they are real! Very real.

River asks me how long this will take.

I snap at her that I don't bloody know. 'The reason we are here is because of you,' I say.

We waited there for over an hour. River keeps asking me, 'How long will this take?'

It's not like I can walk up to the receptionist and say, 'Oh, hi. Look, my daughter wants to throw herself off a building, and my son has just announced that she is now my daughter, so we are in a bit of a pickle here. Is there any chance someone might be able to talk to my daughter sooner? Will that be possible?'

'Come on,' I say to River. 'Let's just go. I will try and get in with your doctor.'

We headed out and go to the car. I ring the doctor's surgery. The receptionist tells me there are no vacancies today. She can hear my teary voice. I am begging her to please get River in to see a doctor today. She puts me on hold and tells me she will see what she can do.

She comes back to the phone and says a doctor will see River in a few hours.

I sob a 'thank you' to her and put the phone down.

I drive River home and tell her I will pick her up for the doctors soon. We are supposed to be leaving to go on the boat this afternoon, but I still haven't got the groceries, and I still have to go and drop Blue off down at my mum's house so she can look after him while we are away.

Jules used to look after Blue when we would go away, but that hasn't happened for a long time.

I don't know how I am going to do all this in the space of a few hours. I rang my mum and told her I can't drop Blue off today, as I have to take River to the doctor.

'What's wrong with her dear?' My mum says worriedly.

I really don't want to tell her the whole story, so I just say that she has been very sad at school and she has threatened to hurt herself. Now I can't stop the tears from coming. I am sobbing into the phone, and Mum says she will come up and get Blue.

'Don't worry, dear. I will come up and get him around 2 pm. Just look after yourself,' she says with a British accent.

I want to tell her the whole story. I want to tell her everything that is going on with the kids, but I can't bring myself to do it. *She doesn't need to know all that*, I think to myself. *Not now. Maybe not ever.*

I go to the shops and get the groceries. I go to the store where I know I won't run into anyone. I do the shopping as quickly as I can and run back to my car. I go home and organise the groceries in the fridge. I grab Blue and put him in the car. I have to just get away for half an hour. I take him to dog beach that not many people go to.

This beach will become my meditational beach for the next few months or so. I know I will never run into anyone I know here. I won't have to explain to anyone what is going on in my world. I won't ever have to tell them that Jules is transgender and River wants to die.

I walk along the beach with Blue. I dig my feet into the sand, almost begging for it to swallow me whole.

I used to love walking along this quiet beach before. I would love the stillness and the way the waves lap at my feet. I would love the way Blue ran in and out of the waves, chasing them like he was playing a game. I used to laugh at him doing that.

'Silly dog,' I would say. 'You are so funny.'

Nothing seems funny now. All I can do these days is cry.

I look up at the sky. It is a brilliant blue without a cloud in sight. It is as if someone is playing a very sick joke on me. 'Why are you doing this to me?' I cry to the sky. 'Why are both my kids so messed up?'

I am looking for signs. Something, anything, to give me an answer to this totally fucked up situation.

I walk and cry, Blue running up and down like he has never seen a wave before and me wishing I was him. Me wishing I was anyone else except me.

I will never get better, I think. *How can I?*

We headed back to the car. I put Blue in the back seat, and he shakes sand everywhere. Usually, I would be cursing him and wiping the sand off him, but now, I couldn't care less.

I turn on the car, and the music starts blaring out of the speakers.

It's George Harrison.

It's 'My Sweet Lord'.

It's the only song I will listen to now. The only song that I can relate to

I listen to every single lyric and scream my lungs out to the song.

I cry, as I scream to the music. Tears are streaming from my eyes. My pain is so raw and so real that there can be no end to it. I will feel like this forever.

My sweet lord.
Hmm, my lord.
Hmm, my lord.

I really wanna see you.

Really want to be with you.
Really wanna see you, Lord.
But it takes so long, my Lord.

Hallelujah
Hallelujah

I really wanna know you.
Really wanna go with you.
Really wanna show you, Lord.
That it won't take long, my Lord.

Hallelujah
Hallelujah

Please lord. Don't let it take long.

I get home, and Mum is there waiting for me with Jules.

Jules looks the same. Same clothes, same hair, same everything.

Mum is talking away to Jules like she is the same Jules she has always known. They have always had a very close bond, and she adores him. Or, should I say, her. How could Mum possibly comprehend what is going on in this household? How could she know that I had just come from the beach where I wished the sand would have swallowed me whole?

I'd wished there would have been a freak wave that hit me so fast that there would be no way I could survive it.

It would have been over in seconds. No more misery. No more pain.

I hear the news on TV in the background. It's all about people dying and people getting murdered. Climate change and bushfires and war. I can't see past my own misery to have any empathy for anyone else.

How is all this going on around me, yet my life is stuck in this place? A place that I can't escape from? A place that has become my new reality?

Mum continues to talk while Jules makes her a cup of tea.

I point to the TV. 'Well,' I say, 'we will all be dead soon I guess so none of this really matters.'

Mum looks at me concerned as if I have lost my mind. *I have lost my mind*, I think.

Mum chats for a while longer and then says she will grab Blue and get going.

'Look after yourself, dear,' she says to me while she gives me a hug. 'I can always help out with River if you need me to.'

What about helping me with Jules? I think to myself as she drives away.

After she leaves, I get River organised to go and see the doctor for her appointment.

At the doctor's clinic, I sit there while River is assessed. I try not to cry as she goes through a questionnaire about suicidal ideation.

She goes through a list of what to look out for and ways I can help River.

Everything that she has asked River in the question-naire, I have answered 'Yes' to.

I am a candidate for suicide, I think. The only reason I don't do it because it will make my family sad.

Hell, they are doing it to me, a voice in my head says.

Kevin gets back from work early so we can get to the boat. I tell him about my day, and he hugs me. I cry again.

I can't believe this is happening in my life.

Kevin helps me organise all the food and puts it in the car.

'It's alright,' he says, 'we can just go and relax over there.'

I don't know what that means anymore. Relaxing is something that I used to be able to do. That word is no longer in my vocabulary.

Jules takes us all to the boat, and I hug her.

'Thanks for dropping us off,' I say to her. 'I am really trying. Please believe me that I am. I just need more time.'

She smiles at me. 'It's okay Mum.' she says.

I wish I could believe her.

GOOD FRIDAY 4 APRIL

There is a little church on the island that Jules and I used to visit every Good Friday and go to a sermon there. We have been doing this since Jules was about eight. I am not really a churchy sort of person, but I always try to go to this church when I am here. It is a small church, and it is so beautiful. It is built high on the hill and looks like it's been there for at least a hundred years. It has been totally unrestored, and I liked to imagine the people going to this church all those years ago. The island used to have a primary school, so I am guessing all the kids used to attend this church also.

I used to look at it like it was a place of peacefulness and joy.

Now, I look at it like it is a place where Jules and I used to go. A place where now I will only associate with sadness. Sadness for a life that I no longer have. A life where everything seemed so good. Now, I cannot see any goodness in it at all.

I tell Kevin, and I am going to go to the sermon. He is not at all a church goer; in fact, he is more like an atheist, but he says he will come with me. River has never liked the church and had confided in us years before that she is an atheist. She has never attended church with me.

'No, I think I will just go by myself,' I say but thank him anyway.

I walk to the top of the hill and go inside and sit at the back on a pew by myself.

There are usually only a handful of people that come to this church. Well, when I have been, anyway. When Jules and I used to come together, I think.

When my life was different…

I sit at the very back of the church. The last pew in the row. I sit alone and cry. I pray to God, and I hope he is listening. Please, God, I cry silently to him. I know we must suffer for our sins, but I cannot deal with this sort of suffering. I am pleading with him. Please bring Jules back to me.

I listen to the priest as he talks about the stages of Jesus death.

1. Jesus is condemned to death.
2. He is made to bear his cross.
3. He falls for the first time.
4. He meets his mother.
5. Simon of Cyrene is made to bear the cross.
6. Veronica wipes Jesus's face.
7. He falls the second time.
8. The women of Jerusalem weep over Jesus.
9. He falls for the third time.
10. He is stripped of his garments.
11. He is nailed to the cross.
12. He dies on the cross.
13. He is taken down from the cross.
14. He is placed in the sepulchre.

I think of Jesus and cry. Is that why I am suffering now, I think? Do we all have to suffer in life for Jesus's pain?

I don't want to be in pain. I want to be dead. Why can't you let me die I beg?

The sermon is finishing, and I stand up and walk over to the donation box. I dropped a $10 note in there. Tears are now streaming down my face, and I have to wipe them away so I can see where I am going.

The priest sees me and walks towards me. He puts a hand on my shoulder.

'It will be okay,' he says to me. 'God will heal you.'

I look at his face. He must be in his eighties. I wonder what sort of life he has had. Has he had pain in his life? Pain like I am feeling now?

I leave the church and go back to the boat. I don't want God to heal me, I think. I want to be with God. I don't want to live in this world anymore, because I can't deal with it. I can't deal with my life.

I go back to the boat and start scrolling again for ways that I can die without actively suiciding. I know that if I do this, Kevin and the kids would be devastated, and Jules will know that I did this because of the situation. That would be horrid. Even though I really want to die, I can't do this to them, any of them. It would destroy their lives too.

I need to find a way to do it without causing any suspicion.

I keep scrolling. Arsenic, mushrooms, berries. *Would any of this be quick?* I think. *Quick enough to not rouse any suspicion?*

I look out at the ocean. I see a pelican. Usually, I would just sit there and watch it, admiring its beauty, but I can't see beauty in it now. It looks just like an ordinary bird. Just like the rest of this place is. Ordinary.

Everywhere I look is just darkness. Dark clouds and endless ocean. There is no beauty in it anymore.

No beauty in the sun that touches my face or the breeze that cools my skin. I feel nothing but numbness and pain.

This sickness consumes my mind and body. It is an all-consuming darkness inside me filling every pore with misery and hopelessness. It makes my head hurt and my body ache and leaves me with a continuous sick feeling in my stomach. It makes me continuously gag and cough. It makes me unable to move. It makes me see only bad in the world. It has taken over the whole of me.

I keep scrolling and find another site. You can put in all your details, and it tells you what month and year you will die.

I answer all the questions, and then I am horrified because it tells me I will be 76 when I die. I feel like throwing the mobile and smashing it into a million pieces. I want it to be now! I want to die now.

I am trying to pretend to read my book as I am sitting there, because I don't want Kevin to know what I am looking at.

He eyes me suspiciously as if he knows what I am plotting to do.

'I might just send a message out to my friends and tell them what's going on.'

I shrug. I know a lot of his friends come here around Easter time, and I guess it's better for them to hear this from us than from someone else.

They all send back messages of support, asking Kevin if we are okay and is Jules and River are okay.

It is so nice to have such support from all our friends and family, but that doesn't make me feel any better.

I keep telling myself that it doesn't matter, as I won't be here for much longer.

We were still on the boat when I get a message from my doctor. It is about a blood test I went for a few weeks ago.

Was this before Jules told me? It must have been.

I have lost track of the time.

Life has been a complete blur since then.

I get regular blood tests because I have a condition called haemochromatosis. It is a genetic or acquired disorder in which iron building proteins accumulate in various tissues. This is then stored in the organs. This can cause damage or even death if left untreated.

The receptionist says the doctor will ring me shortly with my results.

I sit there unable to move or speak. This is it. This is the answer. She will tell me that I am dying. She will say that I don't have long to live. This is the answer to my prayers!

She rings me about half an hour later. I sit there patiently listening to her, waiting for her to tell me that my liver is fucked and can't be repaired.

She tells me that my liver has a spot on it. *That's it?* I think. *Will that kill me, then?*

Obviously, I can't ask her this question.

She tells me that I need to get some X-rays on it and maybe go for another blood test. I won't be doing that.

Maybe it will get worse. Maybe it will get worse quickly.

I remember my mum saying that her friend had the same condition and that she never did blood tests or X-rays or anything for it. 'Then one day she just dies on the spot.' My mum had told me. She told me this while emphasising the fact that I must go and get regular check-ups.

That's too long to wait. I need this to happen now.

I start scrolling and start finding out what you shouldn't take when you have this condition.

You shouldn't have iron tablets, or vitamin C or orange juice, I read.

When we get to the shore the following day, I buy all of these products. I start taking loads of them at a time. I take

10 or 12 iron tablets all at once. I take vitamin C and wash it down with orange juice. I am drinking loads of alcohol every day too. This is my answer. In a few months' time, I should be dead. I hope I will be. Then I would never have to think about this again.

It won't look suspicious at all. Just way too much iron stored in my system. So much that it went to my other organs and killed me.

This secretly gives me some happiness. Happiness knowing that I won't be around for much longer. Knowing I won't have to live in this life while I watch Jules change her body and become a total woman.

The next day, Sandy is coming over to the island with her mum and kids. She asks me if I want to meet up for a drink at the pub. I say okay, even though I just don't know if I can face other people.

We sit and have some lunch, and her mum asks me, 'How Julian is going? How are his studies going? Is he still at university?'

Sandy obviously hasn't told her mum. I answer all her questions but try not to use any pronouns. This is quite difficult, I discover. Is this my life now? Avoiding using any pronouns?

After lunch, I go back to the boat. I take shitloads of vitamin C and iron tablets. I feel like this is a release for me. A small part of me that knows death is upon me and that I won't have to live like this for much longer.

I know in the back of my mind that I should not be thinking this is the way out, but another part of me feels happiness that death will bring me no more pain.

It's a day before we head back home, and I get a phone call from Jules.

'Sally doesn't want to see me anymore,' she says.

'What? Why not?'

'I don't think she can deal with it.'

'She's the one who told you that you were transgender!' I yell down the phone. 'She's the one who said she loves you for the person you are and not the gender!'

For fuck's sake! Now I have this on top of everything else. I feel sad for Jules, but in my head, I am thinking that maybe she will revert to being a boy again. A small part of me is hoping this will happen. If it does, then I won't have to feel like this anymore. I can start living again.

'Can you come home?'

I tell Kevin what's going on. 'It's too windy to head back today,' he says. 'Jules will just have to deal with it.'

In my head, I feel so bad for Jules that I know I must go home.

'I will just get the ferry back,' I say to Kevin. 'You can stay here.'

He knows how bad I have been feeling, and this has only added to my misery. Jules is my child, and I can't deal with her being in pain.

He says we will all go back together, so we put everything away, packed up and head home.

On the way back home, I sit on the back deck and look out at the waves, wishing I could just dive into them and be swept away a long way away from all my pain. Away from everyone and anyone. Away from my existence.

Just as we were reaching the mainland, I got a phone call from Jules.

'It's okay, Mum. Sally's here now.'

Fucken bitch! She is just being a drama queen again. I mean, she's the one who thought this was a big joke, and now she is playing around with Jules's head. I want to smash her fucking face in!

'That's good,' I say. To be honest, I am kind of relieved in a way. I cannot deal with this mental illness now, especially when both my kids seem to have it. It is so exhausting. It seems that every minute of my day is consumed by thoughts of what will happen next and when this will all stop!

Kevin is angry, saying we shouldn't rush home every time Jules has to deal with something. All I can think about is, what happens if Jules takes her own life? That is the worst thing that a parent would have to go through, even worse than what I am going through now. That pain would be unbearable. Even so, my pain is very real. *Not for much longer*, I think. *Soon, I will be dead.* I don't know how, but if I will it enough to happen, then surely it can.

When we get home, they are both there. Jules and Sally. Her ugly face smiling at me as if everything is just perfect again. I can't return the smile. I can't even bear to look at her. She's the one who has brought such misery into our lives. She is the one who has inflicted this pain on me.

I put down my stuff and have a shower.

When I came downstairs again, Kevin is trying to make conversation with them both. I go and sit on the couch and pour myself a drink. This is the first of many for the night.

I sit on the couch and drink glass after glass of wine. I try to focus on what is on the television, but nothing makes any sense to me anymore. I am in a trance. I just want the alcohol to take hold of me so I don't have to think anymore.

I take a sleeping pill and go to bed. Nothing has changed. Jules is still transgender.

I cry myself to sleep and hope I don't wake up. It is a thought that is with me every night as I go to sleep. I keep hoping my heart will fail and it will kill me in my sleep. A broken heart can do that. I am sure of it.

Jules has now changed her name. Not legally, but she has changed it on her Facebook account, at university, and on all her mail.

She gets a lot of parcels sent to our work. I hate other people collecting the mail and seeing her new name on everything. Usually, it's Lego or books or something along those lines. I never used to think much of it, but now, I am grabbing the mail as fast as I can and taking it into my office. I just can't deal with this change of name on top of everything else. It's heartbreaking.

One day when I was at work, a couple of parcels came in for Jules. I race to the counter to get them. I grab them and put them in my office under the desk. All her mail is now in the name of Julie Indiana. Every time I see the name on her mail, I want to be sick. This is not her name. It's Julian, not Julie! That is not the name I gave to her. That is the name that her and Sally decided it should be.

Lucas comes into my office and picks up one of the parcels I had tried to hide.

'Oh,' he shouts out. 'Julie Indiana. We don't know any-one here by that name.'

He is laughing. He is having a joke with one of the other staff members, Sean.

I want to smash the parcel into his fucking face!

I want to pull him to the ground and kick the shit out of him.

But more than anything in this world, I want him to have a kid that one day turns to him and tells him that they are transgender. Then I'll see if he has anything to laugh about.

I say nothing. I am silent.

When he leaves the office, I silently cry.

Those two workers are no longer employed with us. They left our company to pursue other jobs.

I have always stayed in contact with all my ex-workers that leave us to go elsewhere. I have always treated them like they were my own kids. I would buy them coffees on the mornings I was there. I would post their mail and talk to them about anything and everything. I would always show them kindness and respect.

Even now, I cannot bring myself to like these two workers. I try not to see them at all. One of them has a child of his own now. I hope he realises how he made me feel that day. I was already down, and I was suicidal, there's no denying that. Yet, at that moment, he chose to take the knife and dig it in that little bit deeper.

I have one word that plays over in my mind. That word is karma.

I am managing to get through each day, but I don't know how I am doing it. I go to work. I come home as soon as I can. I drink, and I watch TV.

I don't go out anywhere anymore. I like to be where I don't have to see anyone.

My friends are texting me a lot. Sandy, Tess, Chrissy, Rochelle and Janine text regularly to see how I am going.

I lie and tell them all I am okay, but I don't think any of them believe me. I don't want to go out and socialise. I don't want to be with anyone that has a relatively normal life.

I don't want to be here.

WEEK 4

It's the weekend of my sister-in-law Tess's 50th. It is also the week that Jules started hormones.

Tess had been planning this party for months. I tell her I am sorry, but I just can't go. I cannot find any strength in me to be able to even contemplate having fun. Fun is not in my vocabulary anymore.

I think of all the people there that I know who don't know what's going on with Jules, all the people with their perfect families that are not going through what I am going through. They will chit chat and talk about what their son is doing at school and how well he is doing in his degree. They will say their daughter is doing well and starting university. None of them will say, 'Oh, by the way, my son is now my daughter,' or 'Hey, guess who's just started hormone treatment.'

I stay at home. I drink and cry. I will never go out again.

Kevin says he is not stopping his life because of this. He goes to the party. Even though I know his head is full of negative thoughts about what's happening to Jules, he decides to carry on and not give up.

I go to bed at nine with a sleeping tablet and blurred vision from excessive amounts of alcohol consumption.

Kevin doesn't come home until 3 am. He said he had a great time. I wish I could have a great time. I will never have a great time again.

The next night, a couple of friends who know what is going on in our lives texted me. One is my friend Anna. Her boy is a good friend of Jules. They have known each other since kindergarten.

Her words are so kind that they make me cry.

Suze also texts me. She says in time, it will be like the new norm. *Will it ever be like that?* I think. *Will I ever accept Jules as a girl?* I don't think that's even possible.

I text back, 'I wish it was the new norm now.'

Later in the week, Kevin tells me that our friend Paul is coming back to Australia. He lives in England with his wife. They have stayed with us a few times when they have come over here for holidays. Kevin was his best man at their wedding.

His mum is very sick and has only a matter of days before she passes. I feel sad for Paul, but all I can think about is that I have to go out in public to attend a funeral.

Paul has no idea what is happening here.

When he arrives, he comes into our work. I tell him Jules is transgender. I am trying not to cry when I say this.

He is very shocked to hear this. He says he had no idea.

'Neither did I,' I say.

The next week, its Paul's dad's funeral, and I have to attend to show my respects. He came home because it was his mum that was sick, but then his dad passed away first. I know there will be another funeral very soon.

There are people there that don't know about Jules being transgender, but they know Jules from when he was a young boy.

They ask me things like, 'What is Jules up to now?' and 'Is he still at university?'

I don't know how to answer these questions but do the best I can. I pretend that everything is still the same as it was before.

Suze is there with her husband Matt.

She tells me that there is a person at Matt's work who has just come out as transgender. He is now she. I ask her if he is married.

'Yes. He has a wife and two kids,' she says.

'Are the wife and kids okay with that?'

'Yes. He is still married, and the family have accepted it.'

'What about her workplace?' I say. 'Have they accepted it too?'

'Yes,' Suze says. 'They had known for a while that he liked to wear female clothes, but now, he has come out as transgender, so they are using female pronouns.'

They seem very casual about it, I think. Maybe it's because they had some idea that this was going on.

I walk around the gravestones to where the burial will take place. I look at all the plaques and take note of when they died.

Some of these people are only in their forties and fifties. What did they die of? Maybe stress or a heart attack or maybe from a broken heart. Like mine.

Why can't I die? I am pleading with God again. *Why did you let all these people die and you don't let me? I don't want to be here. These people might have fought for their lives. I don't want to so why can't you take me?*

I am looking at the gravestones like these people are lucky to be dead.

I get through the service. It is a sad day for Paul. I try to keep it together.

After the burial, Kevin asks if I want to go for a drink with Paul and some other friends to celebrate his Dad's life.

'I can't,' I say. 'I'm sorry.'

As I walk back to my car, I see one lone black crow. It looks at me.

I have read somewhere that one black crow means death is coming soon.

Follow me, crow, I think. *I am beckoning him to follow me. That will clarify in my mind that I will be dead soon. This is a sign. I know it!*

The crow keeps looking at me but does not follow. *It is still a sign*, I tell myself.

The next day, I am in the laundry, and Jules comes in and sits on the bench.

Jules seems to be at home more than usual these days. It makes me wonder if everything is still okay with her relationship with Sally.

She tells me she went to see her psychologist today.

She has already started to look different. She has just had her ears pierced, and even the way she talks is different. High pitched, almost.

Jules has never had a deep voice, but this is almost put on. Like she is trying too hard. She doesn't need to do that, because the fact is that her voice has always been soft and feminine like. When she worked with us for a while and answered the phones, she would often get mistaken for a female.

'My psychologist suggested that maybe we could go out together for an outing and I would wear a dress and that might help you to accept me.'

'What?' I scream. 'You must be joking! I don't want to go out with you wearing a dress! I can't do that now. Maybe in time, but not yet, Jules. It hasn't even been a month yet!'

'Well, he says that would be the best thing for you.'

'Oh, right,' I say sarcastically. 'That would be fucking great. I guess he's experienced this himself, right?'

'What do you mean?'

'I mean I guess he had a son previously that came out as transgender and is now his daughter, and while this was happening, he had no fucking idea that his son was his daughter, and then a month later, he was fine with it all, and he went out to lunch with her while she was wearing a fucking dress? Is that it?'

'Well, no, I don't think that's what happened.'

'Then how the fuck does he think this will benefit me?' I am screaming now.

'You are just going to have to get used to this,' Jules says and storms off.

I sit there heaving and sobbing and realise it's just another day in this nightmare that I am living. There is nothing I can do except sob. Who are these so-called professionals who think they know everything that should be done in this scenario? Have they ever had this as their reality? As their life? Do they just sit in their chair making up shit that they think would be beneficial in this fucked up situation?

This just makes me sob more.

That night, I left Jules a note at her door. It reads:

Dear Jules

Please believe that each day is going to bring mixed feelings for me.

One day, I seem like I am okay, and the next day, I am not.

This is so hard for me, and I am taking it one day at a time and gaining strength that way.

Please don't keep asking me to accept you like this? I will, and I will be okay.

Just get yourself happy.

Love,
Mum

I feel so guilty after each argument I have with Jules. It is a mixed feeling of anger and sorrow and guilt, but I hate fighting with her. Deep down, I know this is a huge struggle for her, but she needs to realise that I cannot help her unless I am okay myself. She just keeps pushing me to accept this now, and I can't. Not yet. Maybe never. I don't know!

'It would be much easier if you were dead,' a voice inside my head tells me, and I know that the voice is right.

Then Jules can live her life to the fullest as a female, and she would never have to make you try and accept it. She can wear and do whatever she wants. She won't have to worry about her sad, depressed mother. She can be her true self.

MAY 2021

It is well into May now, and I have had over a month of crying constantly every day. Living and breathing this, from the moment I wake up in the morning until the minute I go to bed. I curse God when I wake up in the morning. I curse him for not letting me die.

I still can't eat properly. I constantly gag and feel sick. I don't want to be here. I can't concentrate on anything.

Kevin now has to check everything that I do at work, because I am constantly stuffing up.

My life is a disaster.

I don't think I will ever get well. I will live a lifetime of sickness.

Later in the week, Jules asks if we can get our tattoos done. It is something we had planned long before this happened.

Jules wants a map from *Lord of the Rings*. I have no idea what to get. I don't want to do this anymore, but I say, 'Okay, just book it for us.'

I figure it might be a way for us to get close again. Well, at least for the day, anyway.

When the day comes, I try and get myself together for the outing to the tattoo parlour. I don't want to run into anybody I know. Even though Jules still looks the same, I know that if anyone uses their 'dead name', then it will be an awful situation. For both of us.

Sally has decided to come to hold Jules's hand. *Jesus Christ*, I think. *Why does she have to be around us all the time? I can't even have a day out with Jules without her being there with us!*

I have decided to get a Japanese symbol on my back that reads 'resilience'. If there is some way that I could possibly get through this and live to tell the tale, then I can look back on the tattoo and remember that time in my life. I can't see that happening, though. I can't see myself ever getting past this.

The receptionist calls out our names.

'Jane and Julie?' She looks at us.

I want to fall beneath the floorboards. *Julie?* I think.

I know that is what she wants to be called, but I have never heard it said out loud.

This is such an awful feeling. The name that I picked for my child. The name Julian that I had wanted from the minute I knew he was a boy at birth. The name that I have already tattooed on my ankle. That name is no longer. That name is replaced with Julie. I feel so sick. I am hoping that the tattoo is painful. I want it to be so painful that it can take away what I am feeling inside.

Even as the tattoo artist starts on it, I know that this is not going to take away the pain I am feeling inside. This is just a minor distraction.

After he finishes mine. He starts on Jules's tattoo. Sally sits there holding Jules hand.

I get out of there as fast as I can. I say I will meet them later.

I sit in a café nearby and try not to cry.

I am just holding on here.

How much more can I possibly take?

Jules's tattoo is on her back. She is very pleased with it. It is her first tattoo. Strange, though, because before she came out as transgender, she said she would never get a tattoo on her body.

I have asked Jules not to come to my work. Most of the time, we end up arguing when we are together, and I don't want this to happen at our work. My work is a place where I don't think about this constantly. It is a place of distraction for me. A place where my mind has to concentrate on other things, not just on Jules.

She comes in, and she has a skirt on. It is like she is trying to shove this in my face to make me get used to it immediately.

She starts talking about the car that we are restoring for her. I mean, this car will be worth a lot of money when it's finished. It is an extremely rare car.

She sits down at my desk. I am wondering what argument we are going to get into now.

She asks me about the car. 'What would it be worth?'

'Why?' I look at her.

Then it clicks. She is asking me about it because she wants bottom surgery. That's why she is here.

I can't believe this. 'Why the fuck are you asking me that?' I yelled at her.

Kevin comes into the office and shuts my door.

'What's going on?' He looks at both of us.

'Jules wants to sell the car that you both have been restoring together so she can get surgery,' I say trying to blink back the tears.

'No, mate,' Kevin says to Jules. He still calls her mate like he always does.

'There is no way we are selling that car,' he says. 'If you like, I will buy it off you for ten thousand dollars, and you can have that money, but I am not letting you sell it.'

Jules knows this is not enough for surgery. She would already know how much it is.

'Why the fuck would you come into our work to ask us that?' I scream at her. She looks like she might cry.

'Just go,' I yell at her. 'Don't come back into our work again!'

'Okay, let's calm down,' Kevin says. 'Look Jules, we can work through this, but I don't think it is ideal you come into your mum's office to discuss things like this. You are making her really upset.'

I have started to cry now. I feel sicker than I did before, if that's even possible.

Jules leaves after this, and there was no more discussion about selling the car. There were quite a few more discussions about surgery, though.

I didn't think I could feel any worse than I do now. I thought that Jules might change her mind about all of this. Now, she is talking about surgery. She has only been on the hormones for a month, and now, she is talking about surgery.

When I get back home that night, I research everything possible on gender affirmation surgery. The cost is anywhere from $20,000 to $30,000. I know Jules could never afford that. That keeps my mind from wandering too far. Too costly and too soon, I think. Surely, no surgeon would do that after such a short period of time, I think. It's too risky and is irreversible. *Jules will change her mind before she has the money*, I assure myself.

She has started to be at home a lot more lately. I am trying to stay positive with her around, but we just irritate each other. Every time she asks me about clothes or make-up, I feel like I don't want to know.

I try to help, but I know I am doing it with very little enthusiasm.

She has taken to going out with her friends from school again on Wednesday nights. They usually go for dinner or a drink somewhere.

She goes out with so much make-up on and wearing a dinner dress that it makes me feel uncomfortable. I can't imagine how her friends feel. It's way too overdone. People already think she is a girl, so I don't see why she must go to all this trouble. She doesn't need to when she already looks like one.

Sally never seems to go out much anymore with Jules. It is so annoying for me that when Jules is out, she just stays at home in Jules's bedroom. I wish she would fuck off back to her own house. With her close family who all play a board game on a Saturday afternoon. She is so fucking irritating. I am so glad I have never met any of her family.

On Friday, Jules announces that she is officially changing her gender.

She tells me she has to go in front of a panel of five people so they can decide if she can change it legally.

She tells me she has letters from Sally's friends confirming that she is female. One of them reads:

> *I, William Redden recognise Julie Indiana as female.*
>
> *I have known her as my friend for over a year as part of my daily life.*

She presents as female, and I accept and support her, going forward.

The other one reads:

Hi, my name is Beccy, and I am one of Julie's friends. I first met Julie around April of 2020, when we were introduced by her girlfriend Sally.

They started dating in March, but because of the start of COVID, I had only heard about her and had not had the chance to meet her until a month later.

We have been friends since then and meet out with our group of friends practically every week.

I was one of the first people that they talked to about Julie's transition. I gave my complete support and advice the best I could. I could see the difference in Julie from how much happier she looked to just generally how much more comfortable she was in her skin after coming out. She began presenting female outwardly not much long after. She requested that we use she/her pronouns and chose Julie as a more fitting name.

Julie has been presenting female ever since, from when we hang out at our houses to when we go out.

Our whole group has been supportive and accepting, because we can see that Julie can be herself and present to the world as female. We recently celebrated her official name change, and I hope to be able to support her in whatever aspect I can around her gender confirmation, going forward.

Sincerely,
Beccy McKay

I look at the letters. Like they know her like I did. I have known her for fucking 21 years, and not one fucking sign. This is just brilliant.

What a wonderful parent I must be to not even pick up any of the signs, yet here they are all celebrating her official name change. What a bunch of cunts! Celebrating her and being such great friends with her and helping her, when her mum is not supportive at all.

My life just gets better and better, I think.

A few days later, Jules shows me her certificate that states her gender change. She is now officially a girl.

When am I ever going to get used to this? I think.

It has been over seven weeks now, and I am not feeling any better. I am still avoiding everyone. I only go to work, and then as soon as I get home, I lock myself away. I don't socialise with people. The only thing I do is go to breakfast once a week with Rochelle, and I end up crying the whole time, anyway. I have seen Janine once, and I was very teary trying to explain what is going on with Jules. She could see I was not my usual happy self. I don't think I will ever be like that again.

I don't leave the house on the weekends. The only time I do is to go for a walk with Blue.

Chrissy and Tess have rung me a few times to try and get me out, but I just can't bring myself to do it.

I am going to be crying the whole time anyway, so there is no point.

I prefer to sit at home and wait to die. I am still trying to find ways to do it. I am still taking shitloads of iron tablets and vitamin C tablets so that my organs might decide to put the extra iron in them. *That might take years*, I think, but hopefully not. Hopefully death will come soon.

A couple of days later, I have to take River back to the doctor for a check-up from her previous visit.

I know she loathes me. I am just existing. I am not a parent to either of my children. I can't even help myself, let alone them. I am just existing. That's all.

She starts walking across the road.

'Watch out for cars,' I say to her, trying to keep my attention from straying.

'I don't care if I die,' comes her reply. 'I want to die.'

I sit in the reception area and try not to cry.

I scroll through pages and pages about transgenders and how they have transitioned. This is my life now, just scrolling through pages of transgender stories.

The doctor calls River in. She goes into the doctor's room without me.

A few minutes later, the doctor calls me in as well.

She tells me that I should be more aware of what's going on with River and I should be more supportive of her.

What the fuck? I think. *More supportive? How the hell could I be any more supportive? All I have ever done is try to make both my kids happy. That's backfired. They are both miserable and both hate me!*

I look at the doctor and wonder if she has got a son at home. A son who she didn't know was actually a daughter. I wonder if her son told her yesterday that he is in fact a girl. He told her that he has been feeling like this all his life, but she had no idea.

I wonder if then she would sit there telling me that I should be more supportive of my daughter.

No, of course, that's not going to happen. Of course, it's not, because nobody else is going through what I am going through. Nobody else I know has had a son that has now come out as a daughter after 21 years, and they had no fucking idea! *Just me*, I think. *Just sad, fucked up me!*

I look at her and start sobbing. Not just little sobs. Huge, guttural sobs. I can't stop. I just keep sobbing and sobbing.

She wraps up the appointment quickly.

I go outside to reception to pay the bill, still sobbing.

I couldn't care less if anyone saw me. Anyone that I might know perhaps. Anyone that might ask me, 'Am I the fuck okay?'

River can sense that I am losing it. She sits in the back seat of the car and not the front like usual.

I get in the front. I don't put my seatbelt on.

This is it, I think. This is when I die.

I start shouting at River.

'You want to die do you? Well, I want to fucking die too. Let's die together.'

I start driving erratically. I am speeding up and down the street, not caring where or what I am doing. I am yelling at River while I am doing it. I am screaming at her about how we can both die together. How I can drive us straight into a lamppost and kills us both instantly

She is screaming and crying in the back seat, but I don't want to stop. I want to keep going until we both die. Then we can both have calm and stillness and no more pain.

She is hysterical now. Begging me to stop. Saying, 'Please, Mum, no more. Please, let me out of the car.'

I am like a woman possessed. I keep driving and driving until I am exhausted.

I drive home and let her out. She screams and runs away from my car into the house. She rings Kevin.

He rings me straight away and asks me if I am okay.

'No, I'm not okay,' I say calmly. 'I want to die.'

I start cooking stir fry and start humming to myself.

> *My sweet lord*
> *Oh, My Lord*
> *I really want to see you.*
> *Really want to be with you*
> *Really want to see you Lord but it takes so*
> *long My Lord*
>
> *Hallelujah*
> *Hallelujah*

I cry into my stir fry.

Jules comes home not long after, with Sally in tow.

What is that bitch doing here?

Jules tries to comfort me. 'It's okay, Mum,' she says. 'It will be okay.'

It will be okay if you stop this fucking nonsense, I think. You are the reason I am like this. Just change back to Julian. If you do that then I will be okay. I promise. Just do it for me. You are killing me, Jules.

I keep stirring the cooking and crying.

Sally sits at the kitchen bench looking at me.

She looks at me like I am a worthless piece of shit.

She is probably right. I am a worthless piece of shit.

At least now my family can see that I have gone completely mad. I have gone insane. They will put me away into an asylum. They will give me drugs every day. I will forget who I am, and I won't be in pain anymore.

I can't wait for this. Surely, this proves beyond any reasonable doubt that I have gone completely mad.

When I go to sleep that night, I dream. It is so real and vivid that I am sure it is happening. I can feel it. I am shaking. I am shaking so violently that I know it must be serious. I am dying. This is it. I am having a nervous breakdown.

It feels so good to know that this pain is coming to an end. I welcome it. I welcome death with open arms. I can't wait for this to happen. For me to feel nothing. For me to be with God.

I wake up, and my nightmare returns. *Oh God, I'm alive! No, no, no!*

I can't get out of bed at all now. I lie there crying. I am crying that I am still alive.

Kevin gets up to take Blue for a quick walk. I can't even bring myself to do even the smallest thing, like taking our dog for a walk.

I have hit rock bottom. This is as low as it gets!

I feel even sicker than before, if that's humanly possible.

Kevin comes into the bedroom and tells me it will be okay. It will just take time.

I tell him I never want to leave my bedroom. I never want to venture outside again. I just want to stay in my bed until I die.

'Well, you might want to stop living,' he says, 'but I didn't work all my life to get to this point just to die. Maybe you need to see a doctor or something. You need help, Jane.'

I can't answer him. I just lie there crying.

I texted River, who has already left for school. 'I am sorry,' I text.

'I just want my mother back,' comes the reply.

There is nothing else I can say to make this better. I have already lost my son, and now I have lost my daughter too.

I texted Rochelle and told her I can't come to breakfast as I am too sick.

She texts me back with an emoji. 'I love you so much,' it reads.

This makes me cry even more.

I go downstairs and look for any sort of pill I can take. I have a few expired Valium pills but not enough to kill me.

I drink a few shots of vodka and then take a whole load of vitamin C and iron tablets. It just won't kill me quick enough.

I don't know what to do with myself. I just keep crying and scrolling death sites.

Maybe I can find a local help group? It might be called something like 'The group for mothers that need to be institutionalised because their child has come out transgender and they had no bloody idea.'

Or maybe it might be called 'Mothers who are totally fucked up because of their kids.'

We could all sit around in a circle on our chairs and talk to each other about what life has dealt us and how fucked up we are because of it.

We would say things like, 'Oh, well, that's what life dealt us.'

Or maybe, 'It might get better if we try to stay sane.'

Then we would all laugh hysterically at how miserable our lives are.

'How did we get here?' We would all shriek to one another. 'How did our lives get so fucked up?'

Then we would get out shitloads of alcohol and drink ourselves into a stupor.

Of course, there are no local self-help groups for parents. *That's because I am the only one in this situation,* I think.

I stay like this all weekend. I can just make it outside to walk the dog, but that's all I can manage.

River still won't talk to me, and I don't blame her for that.

There is nothing I can do to make this okay now. Only time will heal this, and I am hoping I don't have much of that left.

Monday comes, and I wake up at 6 am. Seeing the time on the alarm clock makes me cry. I don't want to face the world today or ever.

I am so sad and way too depressed to face anyone.

'Don't worry about coming into work,' Kevin says. 'Just try to get yourself better.'

I stay home but don't know how to make the time go quicker. I can't concentrate on anything. All I can think about is Jules and now River too. They both hate me!

I go for a walk with Blue. A long walk down the back streets where nobody will see me. I focus on some meditational music, but I can't think of anything else except my family and how it is ruined.

Tess came to my work today to see me. When she found out I wasn't there and was at home, she sent me a beautiful bunch of flowers. Kevin must have told her I wasn't well.

She sent it with a card that reads:

> *You can do this, Jane.*
> *You are a strong woman.*
> *You will get through this.*

I cried as I read the message. I am not strong. Chrissy is strong! She lost her husband when the boys were little, and she raised them herself while she worked full time.

I can't even drag myself to work. I am too sick.

A couple of days later, my other sister-in-law Ricky sent me a link to a counsellor she knows well. This counsellor does online sessions.

Ricky has explained my situation, and she wants to book in a time to talk to me.

Ricky is a counsellor herself, but being family would make it too hard for me to open up to her.

A couple of days later, I have my first session. The whole time, I am in tears.

I explain to her that I can't face people asking me about Jules when I'm in public.

She gives me some coping mechanisms.

She tells me if someone asks me about Jules to say that 'Jules is happy.'

She tells me I don't need to elaborate on anything, as it is nobody else's business what is going on in my life.

She tells me to only tell people want I want to know and nothing else.

She also mentions medication.

I hadn't even thought about that up until this moment.

I never thought I would need anything like antidepressants in my life but maybe this could help me.

I arrange for another session a week later.

I make an online appointment with the doctor. The earliest I could get was the following Friday.

We are heading towards June now, and I don't feel any better. I need to do something drastic.

I sit in my car outside of work on the Friday morning waiting for her to call.

She rings and asks me how she can help.

I burst into tears and reply, 'My son has just told me he is transgender, and I had absolutely no idea!' I blubber down the phone. 'I don't want to live anymore! I don't want to be here!'

After a while, she asks me where the nearest chemist to me is.

I tell her it's five mins away.

'There will be a prescription there for some anti-anxiety medication. You can start taking this immediately. This will take the edge of the situation for now. They are highly addictive, though, so it's just short term. You can take up to four a day, but no more,' she says. 'I will book an appointment for Monday for you to come and see me to prescribe you some antidepressants.'

'Okay. Thank you so much,' I manage to say.

I rush to the chemist to get the pills.

Like the doctor said, it takes the edge off immediately. I feel much calmer after taking just the one.

I take four of them that day.

I am still not feeling good, but it's the first night in seven weeks that I haven't cried.

I stay home all weekend and keep taking the tablets. Four each day. It is getting me through, but I know it's only short term.

There are only 20 in the container, so I need to be careful that I don't run out. Just taking that panicky feeling away is making life so much easier. I can see how they would be highly addictive.

I have only been on them for a couple of days, and I never want to get off them.

I go see the doctor on the Monday.

As soon as I get into her office and see her, I start sobbing again.

Explaining everything that has happened with Jules seems so raw. I just can't keep it together. The words come streaming out, like I am a woman possessed.

She prescribed me some antidepressants. I am hesitant, but she explains to me, 'There are times in our lives when we need something like this to make us feel better.'

I sit there nodding.

'They won't kick in for 4–6 weeks, so you have to be patient,' she continues. 'They will work, though, and they will make you feel better.'

I can't even begin to comprehend feeling better, but at least now I have some hope.

She tells me to start off at 10 mg, but if I feel I need more then to go to 20 mg.

She also gives me a couple of repeats for the anti-anxiety tablets. She warns me again that these are highly addictive so to try and not use them all the time.

I leave her office with at least some hope that in a month or so I might feel better. *God, I can't feel any worse*, I think.

Jules has now changed her name legally as well as her gender. She is starting to get electrolysis on her face and body parts too. She is looking very feminine.

It's a week before my mother-in-law's 80th birthday. We have organised to go down South in a week from now for my mother-in-law's 80th birthday.

This has been planned for months, and all of Kevin's extended family and their kids are coming. We are staying in a hotel for a couple of nights and having a big lunch for her on Saturday. This means Jules and Sally are coming. We have already organised an extra bedroom for them.

It gets scarier for me as it gets closer.

I am not ready for this. I am not ready to celebrate anybody's birthday.

I can't get out of this, I think. *I will have to go.*

She rings me at work on the Wednesday. Kevin told her about Jules on the weekend, so I was expecting a call.

'I still love him just the same,' she says, 'He is still your son.'

'He is not my son anymore. He is my daughter. She is my daughter,' I blubber.

I am so upset that I tell her I must go. I have a customer waiting. I am not ready to call Jules my daughter. I don't know if I can ever get used to this.

I have another session with the counsellor.

I tell her I am going down South with the family for my mother-in-law's birthday, and I am not prepared for it at all.

I know that all the family know about Jules now, and everyone has been super supportive, but I still can't adjust to this. Not yet. Maybe never.

She tells me I must focus on getting myself better so I can then be supportive for Jules and the rest of the family.

I know it's true, but when will this reality set in? When will I feel better? I am still in a dark hole, and it feels like everybody is continuing to live their lives while mine is collapsing around me.

The weekend comes, and we head down south. I am extremely anxious and feel sicker now than I did before. I guess I am used to hiding myself away and not having to socialise. This seems such an enormity!

I have my anti-anxiety pills to take, so that brings some relief.

Jules and Sally come down in a separate car.

Jules arrives totally fem. Feminine clothes. Hair done. Make-up on.

Jules's make-up is perfect. She has had her friend's girlfriend give her lessons on how to apply it. She has done an amazing job. Her hair is long and beautiful.

The only part I can criticise is her dress sense. She must have had Sally help her pick some clothes out. They are awful. They don't suit her at all. Sally has the worst fashion sense ever, and now she is helping Jules choose her clothes.

Oh my god, I think. *Could it get any worse? I am trying to come to terms with this, but this is making things so difficult.*

'Call the fashion police,' Kevin jokes to me. I can't even smile, let alone laugh about the comment.

On Saturday, we all gather for lunch to celebrate my mother-in-law's birthday.

Jules and Sally sit down at the end of the table with River. I am glad about this, as I can't confront either of them.

Her cousins are all totally fine with Jules being trans-gender and talk to her the same as they always did. I am so appreciative of this, but still can't help thinking why this had to happen to my child.

I get through the day by drinking a lot of alcohol. I am not better. I am totally irrational now. I have had way too much alcohol, but the pain is still there.

I look across to the cabinet where the anti-anxiety pills are. I empty the container of the little magic pills and count them. There are 13 pills left in the bottle. I have another prescription for one more bottle.

I take a chance. I down the 13 pills and pray to God that this will kill me.

Please, please, please? I am begging him. *Please, let's this do it!*

I wake up in the morning. I am angry. I really thought that might do it!

My sister-in-law had organised yoga.

I text them all and let them know that I won't be going. I don't think they are surprised by this.

Jules and Sally head off, and they take River with them. I am glad that they have all left. River is still not speaking to me, and she really doesn't want to be around me.

It will be hard next week, as the three of us and Blue are going camping up north for three weeks. It's an annual thing that we do in the winter. Jules used to come too until she got too old for it.

I can't wait to go, as where we head, there are no people around. It is a little station that we have been going to for years.

I need to get away. I need to have no interaction with any other humans. I need to be away from everyone and anyone that knows me. Anyone that knows Jules. Anyone that knows how messed up this family has become.

I have one more session with the counsellor before I go. She tells me to try and take one day at a time. Pick something up from the beach to carry with me wherever I go. Something like a shell or a rock. Something that I can keep in my pocket. Something that I can touch every time someone mentions Jules. Something to try and keep me sane.

I go to work and try to keep it together. I have hope now that these drugs might help me. I am still upset all the time and still wish I wasn't alive, but at least I have some hope. A little jar of hope. That's all that is keeping me going. I need this to work. I need to feel well again.

It's a two-day drive to get to where we are heading. I love the long drive, and I try and turn my thoughts to the beauty of the landscape. Every time I have headed up this way, I have always admired the beauty of the red dirt matched with the blueness of the sky and the deep blue of the ocean.

This time, I can't see the beauty. My head is filled with Jules.

I just want these meds to set in, and maybe I will be okay? Maybe?

Within the first few days, River is bored. This is a last-ditch attempt to get her to come camping with us. She is still young, so we really didn't want to leave her at home.

She is driving me crazy. Asking things like, 'How long are we staying here for?' and 'what are we doing today?' The only thing that is keeping all of us sane is her computer. Thank God we have Wi-Fi here.

I, on the other hand, never want to go home. I want to be out here in the bush forever. I will be forever surrounded with the landscape, and I will never have to think about anything again. All I will see is wildlife and beaches and sky. I will never have to interact with anyone again. I will never have to explain to people that Jules is now she.

We decide that it is best for River to go home. She is hating being here with us, and I don't think we have any other option.

Kevin phones Jules to see if she can come and pick up River halfway between where we are now and home.

Jules says it's no problem. She can come and pick River up. COVID is still happening, so we must meet at a certain border of the state, otherwise we are forced to wear masks while we are camping.

Jules is still quite angry with me, and I can't really talk to her much either. I just feel like she is forcing this on me way too quickly.

When she meets us at the border, she is dressed the same way that she was before. It's not a good look.

She has been buying clothes from the op shop with Sally. Not a good idea when Sally dresses like a tramp. Her style is non-existent, and it looks like she has been helping Jules pick out clothes.

'Looks like Sally has been dressing her again,' Kevin comments when Jules is out of earshot. We have some lunch together before they head off. Jules and River gave us a hug. It is a bit forced, that's for sure. River doesn't hug me. She will only hug Kevin.

Jules puts River in the car, and they drive off. She rings us when they get home to say they have arrived safely. I can relax now and wait for those pills to kick in.

I am glad just to be without kids for a while. I need to take time out for myself.

When we get back to the campsite, I go down to the ocean with Blue. I am trying to see the beauty in the ocean. I love looking at it. It usually brings a sense of calmness. Where is that calmness now, I think. It all looks the same to me. It has no meaning anymore.

I look to the left.

On the cliff where the blowholes are is a little plaque. It reads 'Jules'.

I have seen it many times before, but now I really look at it.

Is it a girl or a boy Jules? I think. *Does it matter if it is a girl or a boy? What happened to Jules? What happened to my Jules?*

I reminisce about Jules and all the times we spent together. We would walk Blue for hours when we were camping. We would walk around the rock pools and explore the different crustaceans. We would look at all the shells on the beach, and if they were nice, we would take them back to the caravan and wash them.

We would chat for hours about anything and everything. We would go snorkelling together all the time. We were so close.

What happened to us?

I know Jules has come out as transgender, but I don't think this is the whole problem between us. It's the way Jules did it and the way Sally had to be with Jules to tell me. Why couldn't Jules have just told me? Why does that bitch have to be involved with everything Jules does?

I feel crushed beyond repair. I want Jules back. Not even the boy Jules. I just want Jules. My child Jules. Not this imposter that I don't know. Not this person who thinks I am a terrible mother. This person who thinks that I should be more accepting immediately. This person who thinks that we are not a close family like Sally's family.

I look at the waves and wonder what it would be like just to walk into them and keep walking. I wonder what it would be like to drown.

I have heard people say they have had a near drowning experience, and after the initial shock, they feel a calmness, as if the water is soothing them. Could this be true? Could I do that and pretend that it was just an accident?

Blue would probably chase me into the water barking. He hates swimming, but being a kelpie, he thinks he must rescue anyone that goes in the water.

I go back to the caravan. Kevin is lighting the fire.

We cook baked bean jaffles on the fire, and we drink. I drink a lot. I don't think I should be drinking so much when I am on the antidepressants, but I don't give a fuck.

I have stopped taking all the iron and vitamin C tablets now. They were never going to kill me that quick. I don't think God wanted me to die yet. I think of that saying, 'Only the good die young.' That won't be me, then.

Days pass, and I feel like everything is just a blur. I walk the long stretch of unoccupied beach. Sometimes, I see one or two people, but most of the time, it's just us. Nobody knows me here. Nobody knows that I have a transgender kid and an autistic one too. Nobody knows my past or my present. Nobody knows me or my family. It's just the vastness of the outback and us.

As I walk along the water's edge, I wonder why this has happened to me. Why was Jules born like that? Is it because I wanted a boy when I was pregnant? I mean, Suze wanted a girl, and that turned out fine.

Why was River autistic?

I mean, I did everything right while I was pregnant. I ate the right food. I didn't drink or smoke, and still my kids are so different.

I remember reading somewhere that God only gave you what you could handle. Is that true?

Could I handle having a transgender child? Other people seemed to be okay with it. Why couldn't I?

Maybe both of my kids are born differently for a reason.

The holiday goes too fast, and I am dreading going home. I am not ready to go home yet.

It's been over three weeks already, and I feel like I need another year. The drugs haven't taken effect yet, and I am still not okay with going back to reality.

I am still obsessing with death. I look for it everywhere. It is the answer to all my problems.

Every time I go walking with Blue, I am looking for it.

I see a snake's trail, so I follow it. I am hoping that one quick bite will be the end of me. I won't contain the venom in one spot. I will let it run through my veins and poison my body. I will welcome it. I won't be scared. It will be the perfect death. Just a freak accident.

I see a solitary crow. One lone crow again. *That must mean death is imminent*, I tell myself.

I crave it so badly.

We always listen to talk back radio when we are out camping, and this trip is no different.

One day while we are listening, a man comes on and says he has a secret.

He says his name is Karl. He is an author, and he is from New Zealand.

He says he has a secret to tell. He is a woman. Or, should I say, she is a woman.

Kevin and I look at each other and turn up the volume.

Karl begins to tell us her story.

She says that as a young child, she always wanted to dress up in girls' clothing. Always liked dresses and make-up and playing girly games.

Her dad was a real blokey bloke, as they say. He made his boys tough. Showed them how to fight and defend themselves. Showed them how to play cricket and rugby and anything that was stereotypically boys' stuff back then.

She had two brothers, so she tried to hide it from them. They were typical boys playing rugby and football and getting dirty. Karl said she didn't like doing any of this. She would wait for her mum to go out, and she would hide in the basement of their house and play dress-ups.

She would put on her mother's dresses and her make-up and dance to music in front of the mirror, pretending she was a girl.

She was terrified of being discovered. Back in those days, it was unacceptable to be a boy wearing a dress. I guess it was taboo.

I was enthralled listening to her. I had never really listened to a transgender telling their story. I was too engrossed in what I didn't know about the whole thing.

Karl had a girlfriend. She had been with her for several years, and the girlfriend had no idea that Karl was transgender.

Karl would make up excuses as to why she had to go away and go on business trips. It was a really a way out so she could express herself in other cities. Places where people didn't know her.

She would go to a completely different city where she nobody knew who she was, and she would put on a dress and make-up and go out.

She started doing this more and more, and it became very addictive. She started to imagine living her life as a full-time woman.

Eventually, her girlfriend got suspicious of her constant business trips, and Karl came clean with her.

The girlfriend was relieved that Karl was not having an affair or, even worse, dying of some disease.

She stuck by Karl as she went through all the surgeries required to transition, and Karl eventually starting living as a woman full time. She never changed her name, as she wanted to keep the name her parents had given her. She never changed her voice either. She could have had surgery to feminise and then had speech therapy to start to sound more like a woman, but she decided not to.

When she did tell her parents, she said her father was not accepting of her. Her parents had split when Karl was in her twenties, and she had never seen much of him anyway, so it was no great loss.

Karl said her mother was shocked but then rang a few days later and said, 'Oh. So, I have a daughter now.'

Karl said both of her brothers accepted her as a woman, but it took a while.

As I listened to this story, I was completely intrigued.

At the end of the show Karl said she still looked a bit like a man, but she didn't care what people thought of her. She was a successful author and a good person. She didn't care what anyone else thought.

That night, when we got to the other campsite, I got on to some clothing stores. I ordered a heap of clothes for Jules to arrive for when we got home.

I guess I felt uplifted by Karl's story. She knew she was a woman all along but felt she could not do anything about it. Maybe this was the way Jules felt.

We arrived back home a few days later.

I didn't tell Jules that I bought her some new clothes while we were away.

A few days after that, I received the parcel in the post containing her clothing.

I arranged them on the bed for her for when she got home.

'What are these clothes for?' she said when she got home.

'I bought them for you when I was camping.' I said.

'Thanks so much, Mum. These are great.'

'I didn't want to see you dress like that anymore,' I said 'If you are a girl, then dress like a 20 something girl. Hell, you have the body for it,' I said as I looked at her, 'so you might as well flaunt it.'

I think this was the start of the healing.

PART FOUR

THE HEALING

Jules has started walking in the mornings with me again. Just a couple of times a week, but it's a start.

I am still not okay with everything, but we are starting to talk again.

It's hard when we see people that we haven't seen for a while.

A few people comment, 'Oh my, look how much your daughter has grown!'

I realise they are thinking that Jules is River.

I let those comments go. I don't have to explain this to everyone.

It was a couple of weeks after camping when Jules and I were out walking Blue. Jules is still walking in trousers but has started to tuck. Tucking is a technique whereby an individual hides the crotch bulge of their penis and testicles so they are not conspicuous through clothing.

It is quite a dangerous practice, and I am generally concerned for Jules's well-being.

Jules tells me while she is walking that she has never wanted to be a boy and has hated her penis all her life.

The surgery topic arises.

'I can't talk to you about this now,' I say calmly. 'It makes me feel sick knowing you want to have surgery.'

'Oh, that's fucking great,' she tears into me. 'You are the one who wanted a boy in the first place. You are selfish!'

'it's not because it's that type of surgery,' I explain. 'I would feel sick if either of you kids had surgery. It's just horrible for a mother to have to watch her kid have surgery, regardless of what type it is.'

I can't believe she is blaming me for wanting to have a boy when I was pregnant. I mean, Suze wanted a girl, and I wanted a boy. It's normal for parents to want a certain gender. I mean, we all want a healthy baby, but most of us have a certain preference for a boy or a girl.

'Anyway, I can't believe you are blaming me for that! It's just normal for parents to want a certain gender.'

She storms ahead in front of me. She is so angry at me.

She is angry for me wishing for a boy.

When I reach home, she is already upstairs packing her clothes away.

'I'm moving out,' she says. 'I am going to live at Sally's.'

'Okay,' I say calmly. 'I think that's for the best.'

I am over crying now. I don't feel much of anything. I feel calmer but still a touch angry. I think the drugs have set in, and I don't have much emotion. It's what I needed.

I hate fighting with Jules, but at this point in time, I think her moving out is what is best for the whole family.

River is feeling the tension in the household. It's like we are all treading on eggshells, making sure we are all using the right pronouns and saying the right name. It is a nightmare at times. I mean, we have been using the same name and pronouns for 21 years. It's not easy to just change it suddenly. It takes time to get used to. Time that Jules is unwillingly to give us.

I am sure it's that bitch Sally in her ear, telling her that we are shit parents who are acting like Neanderthals. We are so out of touch with this new reality. We should be more hip and with it and be able to get this straight away.

I don't hear from Jules for the rest of the week. To be honest, I am grateful for the break. I know I need more time to get used to everything, and Jules is just making my life harder, insisting that I should be used to everything by now.

I am getting better with everything for sure. I mean, the other night, I sat down and applied her make-up for her before she went out. Given I was stoned at the time, but I still did it.

Surely that counts for something. Kevin was flabbergasted!

A week later, it is our niece's 21st birthday.

I don't really want to go, but I know that I should, because it is a special day for her.

I haven't spoken to Jules, but I check her bank accounts regularly, so I know she has still been going to university and going out for food and coffee. It sounds slightly creepy, but it keeps me sane.

I am trying not to be angry with her, but I just feel like I am getting blamed for things that I have had no control over. She is giving me some space, but she is not giving me enough time to accept her as a girl. It is getting easier, but it's still very, very raw.

I just need more time.

I don't know if Jules and Sally are going to the party, but I assume they are.

At this point in time, I really feel like I would prefer it if they didn't go. I know we would probably just end up arguing again, and the whole night would be ruined.

When we arrive there, I spot the two of them in the corner. Jules is talking to some of her cousins.

I am staying away. I don't want another fight with her.

I stay in the other corner talking to a few of my sisters-in-law and some other people that are at the party.

I don't make eye contact with Jules at all. I am keeping my distance.

After a little while, she comes over and starts talking to me. She is asking me if I am okay.

'Yes. But I don't want an argument every time we talk. Why do we always come back to the same subject? The subject of you being transgender? Why can't we just talk normally like we did before? Why can't we just talk about your university or what you are studying now or how you are feeling. Why does it always come back to the same thing? Always about gender?'

She nods, and I think she understands what I am saying.

'Maybe I can come back home again?' she says.

'Of course you can,' I smile at her. I miss Jules so much, but it is hard to tell her that when she continually thinks that I am against her.

It's nice just to talk to her without any arguments or any disagreements about when I will accept her for who she has become. It is also nice to talk to her without Sally by her side constantly.

It drives me insane with her always there. Always keeping watch and looking at me like I am this terrible parent who should be accepting of this by now.

At least Jules is dressed nicely. She is wearing a skirt and one of the tops I bought for her. *At least I got that right*, I think.

The following day Jules comes back home.

Let's hope this time we can get along, I think.

I am so sick of all this animosity in the household. Nobody ever used to argue before. Well, very rarely, anyway. Maybe one or two small arguments, and it was usually to do with River. She was the naughty child.

I have started to play squash every week with Sandy. Once a week, we go to the squash court and smash the ball against the wall. It feels good to talk about everything that is going on in our lives and then smash the ball into the wall of the squash court.

Sandy is going through some relationship issues, so between us, we have a lot to talk about.

One day when we were playing squash, she suggested that I should go and see Maree. Maree is a mutual friend of ours, but Sandy sees her more regularly than I do. In fact, I haven't seen her since all this stuff with Jules began.

'Maree is doing all this healing stuff now,' Sandy tells me. 'You should go and see her.'

A few days later, I message Maree, and we organise a meeting.

I feel very calm as I walk into her healing room.

She hands me a card.

It has a picture of Neptune, the Sea God. He is holding up the trident. He is looking across to the mountain where the rough sea stops, and the calm sea is visible.

'This is the card I have just pulled for you,' Maree says.

I start crying. Maybe this is starting to ring true. Maybe I will get there. Maybe I am getting there. I just don't realise it yet.

The healing session is very intense. Halfway through, she tells me that she sees a man there. He is with me always. He has always been with me, and he is the one who looks after me in my present life.

'Who is he?'

'He is your grandfather.'

Both my grandfathers are dead, and I never knew my dad's father. I only knew my mum's. He died when I was eight.

I remember him being a beautiful man with a beautiful heart. I didn't know him very well, because he lived in England, and after we moved to Australia, we only saw him a couple of times.

'Which grandfather?' I ask Maree.

'It's your mum's dad. He says he is sorry that he couldn't be there for you and that he couldn't help you, but he says he is with you always.'

I start crying again.

My Grandad, I think. *He is here with me.*

She plays a song, a song Grandad wants me to hear.

> *When the night has come*
> *And the land is dark*
> *And the moon is the only light we'll see*
> *No, I won't be afraid*
> *Oh I want be afraid*
> *Just as long as you stand*
> *Stand by me*

When I leave Maree, I ask her how much I owe her for her time. She won't take any money from me. I thank her and go home.

I feel a sense of well-being sweep through me.

I feel like a survivor. I am almost starting to feel alive again.

I am not alone. I have Grandad with me.

I ask Mum for every bit of info she has on Grandad.

She asks me why, but I tell her I am just curious, that's all.

I still haven't told Mum or Dad about Jules. I don't feel like I can yet.

I just don't know how to break that news to them.

Jules already has Grandad's war medals. My mum gave them to her a few years ago. She gave them to Jules because she knew that Jules would always look after them.

Mum then sends me a lot of information about Grandad.

I knew he was a Japanese prisoner of war, but then I find out he lost the use of his right hand in the war, and he had to learn how to write with his left hand when he came back home.

Then I learn about his two sisters and his brother. I had heard Mum mention the story a long time ago, but I couldn't remember the facts.

When Grandad was 16 and his brother was 18, they were enlisted to fight in the war. While they were both at war, all of Grandad's three siblings drown. He lost all of them at once. They all drowned together by accident in the lake.

None of the kids could swim back then, and there was no real need for it in England, as it was mostly cold, so nobody ever swam.

The youngest boy was fishing in the lake, and he started to lose his footing. He started to go under, and his sister tried to swim out to help him. She started to drown as well, so the other sister went in to try and help them both.

All three of them drowned.

How did my Great Granny Foster deal with such an awful loss? How could she keep living with such a tragedy?

It sends tingles down my spine.

My Great Granny Foster had lost three children all at once, and the other two were still fighting in the war. I read the newspaper article, and my heart is breaking. How can any parent survive that? How can any parent go on living when they have lost three children in one accident? It is unfathomable.

How strong were my ancestors to overcome this?

I obtain all the pictures I can of Grandad from Mum.

She has started to question why I am doing this.

I tell her I had a healing and was told Grandad was with me. She doesn't ask me why I went to healing, and I am glad for that.

I restore all the pictures I can of Grandad and then place them all around my house. One sits near me on my bed. It is a picture of Grandad holding our old tabby cat that we used to have.

I start talking to him.

He is making me stronger. I know he is. I can be strong. Just like him.

A couple of weeks later, I get a phone call from River's school.

There was an incident in the canteen, and she hit someone. *They probably deserved it,* I think. I know River has been bullied at school, and she is not one to back down. Nevertheless, it is not acceptable.

I go to pick her up.

The school psychologist is waiting at the back entrance of the school for me.

'She doesn't want to go with you,' she says. 'You scared her when you drove like that with her, and she is still really afraid of you.'

'What the fuck' is what I think, but what I say is, 'Well, okay, I guess her dad can come and get her, but I don't know how long he will be, as he is really busy at work.'

I want to tell her to fuck off. I want to ask her if she has any idea what I have been through in the past three months.

Fuck these psychologists and their philosophies and how things should all be a certain way. How we should all be perfect parents who do everything right for our kids. We should always say the right thing. Never smack them. Never tell them off. Never question what they are doing or why they are doing it.

Where the fuck did that get me? 'What about the parents?' I want to scream!

I have two children that hate me and a school psychologist that tells me my child is afraid of me.

Fuck you, I think! 'No worries, then,' I say.

'I will go with her,' River says.

'Are you sure?' she questions River as if I'm not standing right there.

River gets in the car.

I start to drive away, very slowly.

'You are never going back to school,' I say to her.

'Really?' she says. 'Can I do home school like we talked about before?'

'Yes, you can,' I say to her and smile.

I feel a weight lift from me.

Maybe we can be close again after all.

Jules has now returned home. Sally sometimes stays over, but I really can't stand the sight of her.

They are both talking about moving out together. I think it would be best for Jules, but with her, it might not be a good thing. She is the sort of person who cannot leave home. She fears leaving her parents and moving out. I find this quite disturbing. I mean, who needs their parents there 24/7? It's not like she is moving countries or anything. I just don't understand where the hell that girl is coming from.

Jules tells me this while we are walking together.

We are doing this regularly again now, but when we get into a heated discussion about something, we have learned to change the subject now.

We have told all our neighbours now that Jules is transgender, just in case they were wondering why Jules is dressing differently. Not that it matters that much, but I am sure there would be some questions.

Mick across the road is from the Netherlands, so he wasn't shocked at all. He just said that he hoped Jules was happy. He said that every second person in the Netherlands was transgender, so it wasn't a big deal.

In fact, all our neighbours were very supportive, and they all said that they hoped Jules was happy.

Jules's personality has changed dramatically. It's like she has come out of her cocoon and turned into this magnificent butterfly. I am now looking through different coloured glasses. It is almost like I can see the true person she was meant to be. Does this mean I am accepting this now?

I have started to listen to podcasts and audiobooks about transgenders. I have started listening to their stories and how they had to go through so much to get to where they want to be now. Even though I never wanted to believe this was happening to my son, my view has now changed.

I am starting to enjoy her new personality. I mean, she didn't talk much before, but now, she has so much to say.

She has started helping other transgender people at university. She is part of the trans health group there.

I mean, she couldn't even speak in front of a few people before. Now, she is holding discussions and helping people online and speaking out about what she believes in.

She really has become a very confident person.

We have started our casual bickering again.

We used to bicker about silly things all the time when we used to walk together, and now, we are finally starting to do that again. We can laugh at each other. I feel like we are forming a bond again.

It is now August, and I am starting to feel much better in myself and with Jules. I am still not totally together, but I can feel with each day I am getting stronger.

I am at work one day when Melissa and her daughter Gemma come in. I don't ever see Melissa anymore, and there is no love lost there.

I knew Gemma would have told her mother. I mean, that's obvious. I mean, that's why she has turned up at my workplace, right?

Melissa asks me how I am.

What she means is, 'What is going on with Jules?'

She already knows, so why bother asking me.

She says we should have breakfast.

What the hell, I think. Why not. She wants all the gossip so I will give it to her.

We meet up for breakfast later in the week.

When she asks me about Jules, I don't hesitate. I tell her everything she needs to know.

'Oh no,' she says, 'you must be devastated.'

Of course she wants me to be devastated. That's what she wants to hear. She wants to go back and tell her arsehole friends that I am devastated. That will make her life seem so much better than mine. She always thought she was better than me, so this ammunition would be perfect for her.

She adds a few bits into the conversation about the other mothers that are in her bitchy little group.

'Oh, you know Trisha is so broke now. She has no money at all. She is so depressed. Oh, and when the ATAR scores came out, she thought that her daughter would get the best score possible, but Yasmin got higher than that.'

Trivial shit, I think.

She continues, 'Oh, and Gina's son Harry is such an arsehole. He treats her like shit. I mean, Gina is so depressed over there in Sydney, and Harry just treats her like shit. I mean, he says things like I need a new computer, Mum, and you must buy it for me. Stuff like that. I mean, she has no money to buy it for him, because you know they don't have any. Their business went broke, so they have nothing left.'

She tells me this like I am interested. I couldn't give a shit if they are not happy or broke, but I still can't believe she bags all her friends like this.

Anyway, she has all the information she needs now.

She can report back to her bitch friends about how depressed I am, how bloated I look from all the medication I am taking and how my life is pretty much fucked.

They will say things like, 'Oh, poor Jane. She must be devastated. I am glad my kid is not like that.'

They will say this with sympathy. Like they give a shit.

I walk away knowing that I won't see Melissa again.

I won't get a 'How are you going now? Are you okay?'

I won't get a 'Did you want to meet up again?'

I know that she has all the information she needs now. She can walk away and know that she is better than me.

What a fucking bitch. Not one ounce of sympathy there. Not one ounce of caring at all.

I still can't believe that I was friends with these people. I mean, it all seems so insignificant now.

To think that I was upset with these people for ostracising me from their petty group. I really don't care about any of them. I would be happy if I never saw any of them again in my life.

A couple of days later, I see one of the mothers from the group walking down the street. It's Trisha.

I haven't seen her for years.

She was the one who was always nasty about the other mothers and their kids. She always thought she was the best mother and that her kids are the best kids.

She looks at me like she is going to wave.

I pretend I don't see her.

What a cunt

She is still fat. Even fatter than before, if that's possible. I mean, she is fucking huge. She is still ugly too. Even uglier now. How the hell does this woman think she is better than me? I mean, does she have a mirror?

Geez, I wouldn't piss on her if she were on fire. Maybe those fat thighs of hers might rub together and start a flame? That would be pretty funny.

I keep walking knowing that I will never speak to this woman again as long as I live. I am not going to waste my breath on someone that is not worthy of my time.

Maybe I am getting better.

It is fast approaching: Jules's birthday now. It is September. It's been over five months now, and the antidepressants are doing what they are supposed to.

I am getting stronger, and I am now accepting Jules for the person they have become.

The arguments are getting less and less, and they are being replaced by our bickering again.

I am starting to like the new Jules, the one who oozes confidence and is happy to talk to anyone.

I went to see Maree for another session, and I can feel my Grandad is with me all the time now.

Maree has been seeing Jules too. She helps both of us with the transition, and I am forever grateful that she is there at this time of need.

I have begun looking at social media sites again. I start following sites that have 'inspirational quotes' attached.

Some of them say things like:

> *Do not lose hope, please believe there are a thousand beautiful things waiting for you. Sunshine comes to all who feel rain.*

And:

> *Someday everything will make perfect sense. So, for now, laugh at the confusion, smile through the tears, and keep reminding yourself that everything happens for a reason.*

I look at these every day now for inspiration.

I go out for dinner, for the first time in a very long time, with Tess, Sandy and two of my nieces.

Tess didn't ask me to come, as she assumed I wouldn't want to.

I heard her talking about it at our niece's 21st birthday, and I said I would like to come along. She was shocked but pleasantly surprised that I wanted to go out.

After dinner, she tells me that this is the first time that I have been with her after all this has happened that I haven't spent all night talking about Jules. In fact, I didn't mention her at all.

I must be making progress, then.

The weekend of Julee's birthday comes. It is a long weekend.

I am not dreading it like I thought I would, but it does bother me that Jules is classing this as their first birthday. I know it is her first birthday as a girl, but I want Jules to remember all the other birthdays we shared with her as a family.

I used to make such a fuss of Jules at birthday times.

I would have huge birthday cakes and parties with fire engines, farm animals, castles and always heaps of balloons. I would invite all her friends and celebrate big.

I don't want Jules to forget these memories, but I know she is excited to celebrate her birthday as a girl this year. It is kind of bittersweet in a way.

She tells me she is organising two parties this year, one with her and Sally's friends and one with her other friends from school.

'Why can't you just combine them?' I asked her.

'Sally's friends don't like to mix with my friends. They said that they are too rowdy.'

'That's ridiculous,' I say. I shrug and walk off.

Jules's friends are not rowdy. They just like a drink and a bit of fun. God, Sally is such a boring person.

Jules is making such a big deal about which dresses to wear for her parties. It is so tedious that I can't bear it! I must remind myself that she is excited to wear clothes that she wants to be in and not what she has to be in.

She always wore the plainest clothes as a boy, and this is a flamboyant side that I never thought I would ever see in Jules. She was never into fashion at all.

Now, this new Jules is excited about what she is going to wear for each of her two parties.

'I don't know if I can hang around for this,' I say to Kevin.

'Me neither,' he says.

We decided to go camping. Being the long weekend, we make plans to go off the beaten track for a few days.

River gets wind of this and decides to come with us.

She has started talking to me again, and things are no longer heated between us. She doesn't want to stay at home for the parties either.

When the weekend arrives, we say goodbye to Jules and head off. We make sure we go on Friday night to avoid both parties.

Blue comes too, as he hates to miss a camping trip.

We drive out of the city, and in a few hours, we are out in the countryside.

We light a fire and toast marshmallows, and Blue chases the embers.

This camping trip is a lot different to the last one we went on. I am no longer looking for ways to die, and I am no longer sad.

I enjoy the serenity of the solitude of the outback. I look up at the stars that are so vivid in the sky and thank God that I am alive. The sky is so beautiful and clear.

It's Saturday night when my phone starts ringing. It's late, and I'm already in bed.

It's Jules.

'Sally's left,' she sobs into the phone. 'She doesn't want to be with me anymore.'

That fucking bitch, I think. How could she sit there and tell me that she loves Jules for the person she is and not the gender and then up and leave because she can't deal with it?

Jules is sobbing, and my heart breaks for her.

'She says it's too much. She doesn't like me being a girl.'

'Well, maybe you can tone it down a bit,' I say. 'Maybe you can try and look more like a boy.'

As I am saying this, I realise what I am asking of Jules. I am asking her to dress and be more like a boy. Would I want to be told to be more like a boy if I was a girl? Would

I like to be told never to put on make-up or high heels or ever wear a dress again? No, I wouldn't like that at all!

Sally is asking Jules to do something that she doesn't want to do. Jules wants to be a girl. She wants to talk like a girl and dress like a girl and be a girl because that's who she is. A girl.

Do I really want Jules to go back to being a boy? Back to how it was when Jules told me she doesn't want to be here. She doesn't want to live like this?

Do I want Jules to pretend that they are a boy. Could I survive the constant worry of Jules wanting not to be here? The constant worry of Jules knocking at deaths door day after day? Could Jules survive it?

Neither of us can go back to that, I conclude.

'I don't want to tone it down. I don't want to do that,' Jules sobs.

'We will be back home tomorrow morning.' I tell her.

'I don't want to ruin the rest of your camping trip,' she says.

'It's okay, honey. We will be home as soon as we can.'

'Why the fuck does this always happen when we are away?' says Kevin angrily. I know he is worried, but the timing is never great.

When we arrive home, Jules is inconsolable.

Jules is crying at her desk when I get home. No matter how upset she gets, she still manages to study, I think.

She tells me she is not so upset about breaking up with Sally, it's about losing her friendship group with all her friends, the friendships she has forged with Sally's friends, the ones she has been seeing every weekend for the past 18 months.

As much as it angers me, I get on the phone and call Sally. I asked her if she can talk to Jules.

I don't know what was said, but Jules was no happier after the call.

'Who would ever want me?' she cries. 'I'm a freak!'

If I ever felt my heart break, it was at that moment.

My child was in pain. My baby was in pain. I feel sick to my stomach. It is unbearable to watch.

That fucking bitch Sally. If she was in arms' reach, I would strangle the cunt!

'You are not a freak, honey. You are smart and beautiful and caring. Who would not want to be with you?' I say to her through tears as I hug her for a very, very long time.

I never hear from Sally again, and I am glad about that.

She made me feel uncomfortable, to say the least.

Jules is still in the same chemistry class at university as her, and she hates every minute of it.

They are both heading towards scholarships at the end of the year, and I am praying that Jules gets it and she doesn't.

Jules and I are walking together again daily now. Once Sally was out of the picture, I really started to enjoy her company again.

My friend Janine's daughter Dani has befriended Jules and introduced her to her circle of friends. I couldn't be more grateful to her.

They haven't connected since they were little, and Jules is revelling in being part of a group of girlfriends.

Jules has a lot more time on her hands now, and so she decides to look for a part-time job. Just a few hours a week while she studies.

The topic of bottom surgery has come out more than a few times now, or the correct term being gender affirmation surgery. I have read about a lot of people that have gone down this path, and it has improved their quality of life. We are hoping that Jules is making the right decision.

Kevin and I have discussed this, and both of us agreed that if Jules wants to go down that path, then she needs to save up for it. It's not that we are against it, but if there were any regrets, we don't want it to come back to us.

This is Jules's decision and her decision only.

I am apprehensive, but what is the alternative? Jules tucking all time? That's dangerous enough as it is. It can cause urinary tract infections and twisting inflammation of the testicles, along with a heap of other ailments. Either way, I want Jules to be happy now.

Whatever she decides we will both support her. I mean, she didn't ask to be born this way, and she is not doing this to piss us off. She is doing what she needs to be a complete woman.

In the short time I have had to get used to this, I think I am starting to understand that Jules needs to be a woman. It is not a want but a need.

She ended up getting a job at a local fish and chip retail store. It is a huge store with heaps of people that work there. It is busy all the time, so Jules is picking up heaps of shifts.

She has researched the surgeons that perform this type of surgery, and there are only a handful of them in Australia. The one she wants, or the one that she feels would be best for the job, is in Canberra. There is a two-year waiting list.

I am thinking that she might change her mind, but Jules is so determined that I have decided that this won't be the case at all. She will do it, and it's just a matter of when.

I go into the shop one day when Jules is working, and I ask one of the assistants if Jules is there.

'Oh, you mean Julie?' she says.

'Yes, Julie' I say.

163

Every time I hear that name, it reminds me of Jules and Sally sitting there and giggling while they tell me that Jules is transgender. I don't want her to have that name. That is not the name I would have chosen for her at birth.

When she got home that night, I asked her if she could change her name again.

'But Mum, it took me so long to get this name organised. The driver's license, birth certificate, university. All that shit I would have to change again.'

'I know, but it reminds me of you and Sally and when you told me. It broke my heart, and every time I hear that name, all those memories come flooding back to me.'

'What do you want me to change it to?'

'Juliette' I say. 'That would suit you better.'

She agrees that she will do this for me. I tell her I will pay for the change of name fees and any other costs that are involved, but I would like her to do this as soon as possible.

Within a couple of weeks, her name was changed to Juliette.

I am much happier with this name, as at least I know I chose it for her, not her ex-bitch girlfriend and their family.

We are in November now, and I am feeling one hundred percent on what I felt like before.

I still have a few people question me about how Jules is doing. Some of these people don't know Jules is transgender, and they use her dead name of Julian.

I no longer burst into tears. I answer, 'Yep, Jules is good.' That's all I need to tell them. They don't need to know the whole story.

People who know me and know what I have been through and still going through do not question me. The people who do only want gossip.

I have told the people that I trust and that I know care about me and my family. That's all I need to do.

Jules has arranged to get feminising chondrolaryngo-plasty in the third week of November. This is also known more commonly as 'tracheal shave'. It improves the neck appearance of trans women by effectively reducing the prominence of the Adam's apple.

I hadn't even known this surgery existed. Moreover, it is covered by the government scheme, as it is not classed as cosmetic surgery.

'Can you give me a lift up to the surgery?' Jules asks me the day before the operation.

'Of course, I can,' I say. 'I really don't know why you need this done though. You don't even have an Adams apple.'

This is true. Jules doesn't have an Adam's apple. I guess I never noticed this before. Her Adam's apple is barely noticeable.

'I just don't want anything there that even comes close to looking like one,' Jules says.

The day of the surgery comes, and I take her up there and drop her off at the door. I give the nurse my details to ring me when she comes out of surgery. It is a day proce-dure under local anaesthetic.

At 3 pm, the nurse rings me to say Jules is ready to be picked up.

When I got there the nurse told me to take a seat. Ten minutes later, Jules comes out with a huge bandage wrapped around her neck. She is also totally spaced out on drugs.

'He needs to take three of these tablets a day and the antibiotics. If he needs pain killers, then take one of these, but no more than four a day,' the nurse tells me.

I am a bit taken about. Why is she using the pronoun 'he'? I mean, Jules is in a skirt and just had surgery to get rid of her Adam's apple, and she is saying 'he'?

Jules, in her drugged-out state, picks this up. 'Why is she saying "he"?'

I try to ignore all this and just get Jules out of there as quickly as possible.

I go across to the chemist and get all the drugs that have prescribed.

I leave Jules in the front passenger seat to wait while I go in.

She is in a lot of pain and vomiting into a bag when I return but keeps saying, 'Why did she call me "he"?'

'You're delirious,' I say. 'She didn't say that.'

It wasn't until a couple of years later that I told Jules she did say 'he'.

Sandy and I are playing squash one week when she mentions that one of our friends or more acquaintances from primary school has a child who is going through the same thing that Jules is.

'Really? Who?'

'Karen. Her son has come out as transgender, and she is going through the same thing as you are.'

I know Sandy is not saying this as gossip. She is telling me this to see if I want to reach out to Karen.

I know Karen by association. We have been to a couple of events together with other people.

I know that she has two boys who are twins, and they are both autistic. They would be around 17 by now.

'Do you think I should message her and arrange a meet up for a coffee?' I ask Sandy.

'Couldn't hurt,' she says, as she smashes the ball against the wall again.

A week later, I texted Karen.

'Hi Karen. Just thought I would drop you a line. Apparently, my Jules and your Ash (Ash is the fem name now) are going through the same thing at the moment. I was wondering if you might want to catch up at some stage?'

I got a message back from Karen the same day. I know she is a social butterfly, and she is always going out. Unlike me. I am Facebook friends with her and see her posts come up all the time.

'That would be great,' she responds.

I organised a time for her and Ash to come around for a drink one night the following week. She lives around the corner from me, so it works out well.

When she comes around the following week, she is shocked to see Jules.

'Oh my gosh,' she gushes. 'Jules, you are so beautiful.'

'Thank you so much,' Jules says.

I couldn't have put Jules into this scenario a year ago. She would have just sat there and said nothing. Now, I can't shut her up. She talks and talks and talks some more. The change in her is phenomenal.

Ash is still not old enough to go onto hormones and is still waiting to transition and is not used to being in social settings.

Of course, I know about these kids because River is the same.

Karen works for a large company and is one of the head spokespeople for the trans section of the company.

This is much bigger than I thought. These trans communities are everywhere.

We share a bottle of champagne and talk about all sorts of things.

I listen to Jules talk about her studies and what she hopes to achieve in her life, and I feel proud of her.

It can't have been easy doing all this and transition-ing at the same time. Most people would fall into a heap, but she has really surprised me with what she is achieving now and what she could achieve for the future.

She is not embarrassed of who she is. She is proud of who she is, and finally, I know that I am proud of her also.

At the end of the night, we say goodbye and arrange to meet another time.

Karen says there are a few events coming up with the trans health community that she runs and suggests maybe we could catch up for one of those.

'Why not,' I say. 'Sounds like fun.'

We are heading towards Christmas now, and I still can't bring myself to tell my mum and dad. I just don't know if they would understand.

I have been listening to a lot of audiobooks and pod-casts of parents of transgender children, and I can't believe how strong they are.

One woman says, 'Well, it's how they were born. They don't want to be like this. They just are like this, and we need to support them.'

She then goes on to say that not all her family accept that her son is now her daughter, but she doesn't care. She says she just won't see them anymore. After all, her child is the main priority here.

I listen to the words and try to gain strength from what she is saying. I know she is right. I should be able to tell my parents, and if they judge Jules, then that's it. I just won't see them anymore. *Easier said than done,* I think. Jules and my mum have such a lovely relationship that I don't want to spoil it. I know my mum would probably understand, but my dad is very old-fashioned.

Kevin thinks that my parents will be fine about it all, but I am still apprehensive.

A few weeks later, I went out with Karen. Jules and Ash come along, and Jules is a hundred miles an hour as usual. Talking nonstop, which is good, because Ash is very quiet and reserved.

We went to a film, and it's called *Dawn, Her Dad and the Tractor*. It is an event for the trans community, and the film is about a boy who is trans and is now a girl. She goes back to her little country town, where people are not familiar with transgender people and are very sceptical about it.

In the end, her dad accepts her for who she really is. It is quite an emotional story.

It wasn't so much the film that intrigued me. It was meeting all these people who were transgender. They were all lovely people, and I couldn't get over all the struggles they faced when they came out, not just with their families but with the wider community.

These were people who had good jobs. They were good community citizens. Their only difference per se was that they were transgender.

It's not like they were meth heads or criminals. They were good, upstanding citizens of the community, yet they were being treated like they had some disease.

I felt so sad for these people. I know it would have been a struggle for their families to get used to this. I mean, hell, I struggled. A lot! But to never talk to your child again because of them being transgender is another story.

I was glad to be there with Jules and be supportive of her.

I know I have changed a lot in the past six months, and I am a much better person for it. I am also a lot more aware of people around me and how they might be suffering.

I caught up with Karen and Ash again a couple of times. It's nice to talk to someone who knows exactly what I am going through and what Jules is going through too.

One night, we all went out to a pride gathering with a lot of very interesting characters.

I feel like I have been introduced to a different world full of interesting people who really don't give a shit about what other people think of them.

I am surprised how Jules is so open to people about her transition. It's like she is a different person altogether. She is so confident speaking to other people, and socialising is not an issue with her anymore. As a boy, she found it very hard to socialise or make conversation with anyone. This new Jules is a shining light. Holding her head high and living her best life. It is an amazing transformation.

As my birthday approaches, I realise my mindset is completely different to the last birthday. I have literally made it through a year of hell.

This time last year, I was in a complete hole thinking Jules might take her own life. This year has brought me so much pain, but now I am beginning to look at things in a new light. Jules is a girl, and she is amazing! I don't have to feel sad and depressed about my child being a girl anymore, because I can see her for the person she truly is—a beautiful, smart, caring person. My beautiful Jules. The same Jules but with a completely different personality.

I know I have a long way to go, but right now, in this moment, I can truly say I am so very proud of Jules and how she has handled herself in this unique situation.

A few months ago, Rochelle had arranged for me and a few other people to go down to her holiday house for my birthday. At the time she organised it, I had said yes, I would go, but I remember thinking that I hoped that

I wouldn't be here now. I had hoped back then that I would be dead by now.

We headed down there for a few days, and I am surprised that I had such a nice time.

A couple of the girls I went with had only just found out about Jules, and they were so supportive. I even found myself laughing. That's something I never thought I would do again.

I have known these girls for a long time, right from when we all started to have babies.

We went out for lunch and talked and drank champagne on the beach.

It was the first time in a very long time that I felt relaxed and wasn't constantly thinking about what was happening with Jules.

It's not that bad, I thought. Jules is a great person. It is hard to call her my daughter, though. I guess that comes with time. One step at a time.

The last time we were here was when Jules started seeing Sally. It seems a lifetime ago now.

Thank God they are not together anymore.

'Mum, I got the scholarship!'

'Oh my God!' I give Jules a big hug. 'You are amazing! This is fantastic news!' I shriek excitedly.

I am truly happy for Jules. She has worked bloody hard to get this scholarship, and she deserves it more than anyone else I know.

'Did that bitch ex-girlfriend of yours get one?' I say to her.

'I don't know, Mum. I don't really care.'

'You're right, sweetie. I don't care either. Let's have a drink and celebrate!'

I am so excited for Jules. I mean, how many people can go through all that shit that she has been through and still come out at the top of their game with a scholarship? It is really an amazing achievement. She will be on her way to becoming a Doctor of Chemistry now and without the expensive HECs fees.

We ring Kevin to tell him. He is as excited as us but says he always knew Jules would get one.

XMAS DAY 2021

Jules is excited to wear a dress for Christmas. I guess it's a huge thing for her, as for the past 22 years, she has always been in shorts and a baggy shirt.

She has a red dress for the occasion.

There is just one hiccup. She can't wear it when Mum and Dad are around.

I still haven't told them.

We have breakfast at our house, and it's just a small gathering of people.

I have asked Jules to be in 'Boy mode' when my parents come around, and she has agreed.

She looks casual in shorts and a T-shirt when my parents arrive.

Neither of them looked at Jules any differently than before. Rochelle is also there and must correct Jules when her 'girl voice' comes out.

'Boy mode,' Rochelle says to Jules.

'Oh, right.' She is giggling.

I am thinking to myself that this secret can't last for much longer. I will need to tell Mum and Dad.

When we go to lunch at my sister-in law Chrissy's house, her dress sense and mood changes completely.

She has on a red dress and is socialising and talking to everybody there.

A year before, she would have been dreading Christmas day, but now, she is loving it. I guess she is being her true self.

JANUARY 2022

Jules has put herself out there on Tinder. This makes me very nervous, as she is putting herself out to boys as well as girls.

'Make sure you put in there about you being transgender,' I tell her.

I am truly scared that she might date a boy who has no idea, and then he might get angry at her for not telling him.

'I have,' she says. 'It's all in my profile.'

I am still very worried that someone might overlook that part.

She goes on a date with a boy but then afterwards tells me that he didn't realise she was transgender.

'This is what scares me,' I say to Jules. 'You just don't know how people will react to you being transgender.'

A few weeks later, she comes home with a girl.

She introduces herself to me when she comes through the door.

'Hi. I'm Shelby.' She extends her hand out to me.

'Hi. I'm Jane.'

I warm to her instantly. She is so chatty, and I feel like I could easily get along with this girl.

She also seems besotted with Jules.

FEBURARY 2022

I have decided to tell Mum. I have listened to a lot of audio-books of parents of transgender kids, and it has given me courage to speak out and tell her.

I tell Jules that I am going to tell my mum and dad, and she seems a bit reluctant.

'Do you think they will be okay with it all?' Jules asks me

'I don't know,' I tell her. 'I hope so, but I don't really think they will understand it.'

'Are you sure you want to tell them, though?'

'I will just tell your gran for now. She can decide whether she will tell your grandad or not. I mean, how long can we continue to hide this?' I sigh. 'How long can you keep pretending to be a boy?'

'Yeah, I guess you're right. When are you going to tell them?'

'I will text Gran and will go to see her on the weekend,' I say. Jules looks more nervous than I do.

I arrange to go and see my mum the following week-end. I texted her that I have to tell her something about Jules. I ask her if we can just meet without Dad being there. I don't think I can handle telling them both together, so we arrange to go out for coffee.

'Okay,' she texted back. 'I will talk to you when you come down here.'

I go to see her the following Saturday.

'Is Jules gay?' she asks me when we get in the car to go out for coffee.

'I wish that's all it was,' I say to her.

We stop in the carpark of the shopping centre, and I turn off the engine.

'Jules is transgender,' I explain to her. 'She is more of a female than a male.'

I say it in a way that it is not so dramatic. I don't just want to say, 'Hey, Mum, Jules is really a girl.'

I cry as I am telling her. I explain how hard it has been for me and for all of us. I tell her I had to go on antidepressants, as I didn't want to live anymore.

She holds my hand and starts crying.

'Why didn't you tell me before?' she says. 'I could have helped you, dear.'

'Nobody could have helped me, Mum,' I say through the tears. 'I could hardly help myself.'

'Are you going to tell your dad?' she asks me.

'I can't, Mum. It's up to you if you think you should. I just don't know if he would understand.'

A few days later, Mum texts me to say she has told my dad, and he is okay with everything. I feel so relieved that I have finally told everyone I know about Jules. There are no more secrets to hide. Jules can be her true self around all her family and all our friends. It feels like a huge weight that has been lifted from my shoulders.

MARCH 2022

Kevin and I have headed back to our favourite island getaway for Easter.

It has come early this year, but this time, I feel completely different from how I did last Easter on the island.

On Good Friday, I go up to the church for the sermon, and this time around, I am praying to God to thank him for not letting me die. I thank him for giving me strength to carry on. Now, I can be here for my children and help them through life's struggles and triumphs like I promised to do when I gave birth to them.

We are going for our morning coffee when Jules rings me. She is crying.

'Mum, I don't have any sperm left so I can never have biological children,' she cries down the phone.

I knew Jules was going to try in a last-ditch attempt to see if they had any sperm left so she might be able to have a biological child. It might have been that the hormones made that not possible, or it could have been that Jules had not much of a sperm count anyway.

Either way, I can't bring myself to listen to this. In less than a year, Jules has gone from saying she never ever wanted children to now when she has decided that she might want to.

'We had this conversation, Jules. You said you never wanted kids, and I said you were probably too young to make that decision.'

'I know, but I have changed my mind now,' she sobs.

'It's too late, Jules,' I say firmly.

I hand the phone to Kevin to speak to her. In my mind, I am crying for Jules, but I can't take this anymore. I love and care about Jules so much, but the vision of Jules standing there telling me that there is no way she ever wants kids just over 10 months ago to what she is saying to me now on the phone is something that I have no words for. I cannot bring myself to say any words that will make this better for her. It was her decision at the time, and she will have to deal with it that.

Kevin gets on the phone, and he is saying some calming words to Jules. 'It's okay, Jules, you can always adopt children. There are plenty of unwanted children in this world, and maybe that's what you are meant to do in this lifetime to help one of them.'

The words that Kevin is saying to her are so true. There are a huge number of kids that need adopting now, and maybe that is what is supposed to happen with Jules. Maybe she needs to adopt a child one day.

THE RECOVERY

'Mum, they have a spot for me in May. Someone has cancelled.'

'Cancelled what?' I say, confused.

'For my surgery,' Jules says excitedly. 'In Canberra. I can get it done in May.'

I don't know how to feel about this news. I knew it was coming, but I didn't realise it would be so soon. It has been just under a year since Jules started taking hormones, and now the date of the surgery is about to be confirmed.

Jules is talking excitedly about it, but I am sitting there wondering how to feel about this. Six months ago, I would be bawling my eyes out begging Jules to not do it. Now, I am thinking that is the only thing she needs to do to make her a complete woman.

She has worked hard and saved most of the money needed for the operation, and the time has come for this part of the journey to happen.

I text Rochelle and tell her that a date has been set for Jules's surgery.

'I'm coming with you,' she texts back.

I am so relieved, as I need the support of a friend. Kevin and I both can't take two weeks off work, so it will be me that is going with Jules to Canberra.

'Oh, that would be great,' I text back Rochelle. 'Thank you so much.'

The date is set for the 14th of May. The surgeon is specialised in gender affirmation surgery and is one of the best in the country.

I am so nervous for Jules, but I know this is what she wants. I am glad that I can be there to support her.

'Shelby wants to come with us,' Jules tells me.

'Are you sure? I mean, this is a major operation. Are you sure she knows what she's getting herself into?'

'Yes, she does, and she is fine with it.'

Kevin organises the accommodation, so we are in walking distance of the hospital. We have booked the Airbnb for two and a half weeks. Jules needs to stay there for at least 10 days after the operation, in case there are any signs of infection.

I am grateful that Shelby and Rochelle are coming. I really don't know if I could deal with this alone.

Shelby says she will stay there for the extra 10 days while Jules is recovering. I couldn't be more grateful to have her there.

MAY 2022

Shelby and Jules fly in a few days earlier to meet and talk to the surgeon.

Rochelle and I get there a day before the surgery.

The day arrives, and Shelby and I walk down to drop Jules at the hospital. I feel completely numb. This is my baby who is going in for an eight-hour long surgery, and just as I thought, I feel sick to my stomach.

We hug her, and she walks through the sliding doors that will lead her to the reception to book herself in.

I say a silent prayer to God. *Please let her be okay. Please let her get through this, God.*

It is one of the worst things for a mother to have her child undergo surgery and then wait for the outcome, especially with this type of surgery that is relatively new. I think the surgeon has only done this with about 20 patients, but they have all had successful outcomes.

We decide to go out for the day while the surgery is happening. I have been given a number so I can check on my phone for any updates and for when the surgery has been finished and Jules will be in recovery.

As the five-hour mark approaches, I am getting very nervous. I keep checking every ten minutes. I can't think of anything else other than my baby being okay, that this surgery has been a success, and she is in recovery.

It gets to five o'clock, and I check again. Finally, Jules is out of surgery and is okay and in recovery.

'Oh, thank god,' I say to Shelby and Rochelle. 'She is in recovery.'

'Champagne?' Rochelle asks me.

'Give me ten bottles.' I laugh.

I ring the reception at the hospital, and she tells me that we can go and see Jules in a couple of hours.

'She will be pretty groggy but should be okay with visitors,' she tells me.

Rochelle goes back to the apartment that we are staying at, and Shelby and I head to the hospital.

There can only be one visitor at a time, so I go in first.

'Jules?' I say, going over to her and stroking her hair. I am so relieved that she is okay and in recovery that I nearly burst into tears.

The male nurse is in the room and looks over and says to me, 'Oh hi, I'm Greg. You must be Juliette's girlfriend?'

I start to giggle, 'No, I'm her mother.'

'Oh, you look so young, I thought you must be her girlfriend,' he says.

I guess I know he is joking, but I am loving the compliment.

Jules pipes up then. 'Oh, it's always about you, mother!'

She is heavily drugged and in her own little world, so I don't take offence.

'No, it's not, honey. It's all about you and how well you are doing.'

'Whatever,' she slurs. 'I am a girl now! A complete fucking girl!'

'Yes, sweetie. You are a complete girl now.'

After about half an hour, I send up Shelby. She is desperate to see Jules, and to be honest, I have had enough of the drugged, slurred insults.

I tag Shelby in and text Rochelle to say I am on my way back.

'How is Jules? Everything okay?' she texts back to me.

'She's fucking annoying,' comes my reply.

Jules spends the next week in hospital. Rochelle stays with us for a first few days and then flies home. She goes to see Jules in hospital before she leaves. Jules is happy to see her and thanks her for coming over and supporting us all.

Jules was her godson and now she is her goddaughter. I can say that easily now.

I stay for the week and go and see Jules in the hospital every afternoon. I usually only stay for half an hour or so, but Shelby stays for the whole afternoon with her every day. I couldn't be more grateful to Shelby for being there for us all when Jules was recovering.

Shelby stayed there with Jules for the whole two weeks.

Jules got out of hospital on the second week but had to remain in Canberra for the next eight days to make sure she healed okay.

She contracted an injection in the second week, but luckily, the doctors and nurses at the hospital looked after her and put her on the correct dose of antibiotics to recover.

JUNE 2022

'Cheers!' We are all out to dinner to celebrate Jules.

We all toast our glasses to her. She looks absolutely perfect as a girl. She is wearing a beautiful flowing dress with a jacket to match, and her hair is long and loose. Her make-up is perfectly applied. She looks beautiful.

'Well, hopefully, you will be happy now,' I say to her.

'I am happy, Mum,' she says, looking at me smiling.

I look back at my clever, amazing daughter and smile back at her.

EPILOUGE

I have written this book knowing that it might offend a lot of people. That was never my intention. I wanted people to get the perspective from a parent's point of view on how much their life changes when their child comes out as transgender.

It is not an easy journey for the transgender person, but it can be just as difficult for the parents of that child.

My journey might be very different to other parents' journeys, but it has been a long road to recovery for both me and the family. It was something that I thought would never happen to me or to my child, and I guess I could be seen as quite ignorant about the subject of what it means to be transgender.

I think the hardest part for me was that I had no idea that Jules felt like that, and because I had no idea, I thought that it mustn't be true.

I have grown very close to Jules again. Jules is living in Melbourne happily, and I talk on the phone to her most days.

She was offered another scholarship to La Trobe university for $50,000 per year to finish her doctorate in chemistry.

The Catholic boy's school that she used to attend ostracised her completely when she came out as transgender. She used to go back to that school and talk to the students on how to learn new study habits. She also used to tutor students there for free after school when she was attending year 11 and 12 and doing her ATAR.

Even though she was chosen for the 'Edmund Rice Award' by all the kids in her year and was the third highest ranked student of her year, the Catholic school did not want her to come back because she is transgender.

She wasn't ever acknowledged by the school for the academic achievements she has attained. If she wasn't transgender, she would have been on their quarterly handbook, probably on the front page, so they could show everyone what amazing boys they produce from their school.

Jules has become the girl she wanted to be, and a beautiful one at that, not only on the outside but inside too.

She continues to study hard and has just passed the GAMSAT test to get her into medicine and help people who are also trans after she finishes her chemistry degree.

She has a passion to help people, and I know that she will succeed in whatever she puts her mind to.

She is beautiful, intelligent, caring, and she is my daughter.

It was she who suggested that she might want to write a book about her journey. I jumped on the bandwagon and decided to write my own.

ACKNOWLEDMENTS

Thank you to all my true friends and family who have been there and supported me when I was at my lowest point in my life.

Rochelle, Chrissy, Janine, Tess, and Sandy for the hours of listening to me cry and vent. Also, to my other beautiful friends who have supported Jules and the family and have never said a negative thing about our situation (you know who you are). You are forever in my heart.

To my family, for accepting Jules as transgender and supporting her and for also supporting us. It couldn't have been easy.

Thank you to my husband Kevin, who is the calmest person you would ever meet. To go through seeing me at rock bottom and seeing all our lives changing, you stayed calm and committed to the family. You are my rock!

Lastly but not least, a huge thank you to my beautiful Jules. You helped make this book possible. You have had such a huge impact in other people's lives who are going through what you are going through and gave me inspiration to write a book to help other people that might be going through what I went through. You are an amazing human being!

Milton Keynes UK
Ingram Content Group UK Ltd.
UKHW021004211124
3009UKWH00036B/122

9 781923 163522